The Beatitudes
Bible Study

Taking the Beatitudes Message
to This Generation

Marlin J. Harris

WESTBOW
PRESS®
A DIVISION OF THOMAS NELSON
& ZONDERVAN

All Scripture quotations, unless otherwise noted, are taken from the Holy Bible, New International Version®, NIV®. Copyright 1973, 1978, 1984 by the International Bible Society. Used by permission of Zondervan. All rights reserved.

Scripture quotations where noted (NASB) were taken from the New American Standard Bible. Copyright 1960, 1962, 1963, 1968, 1971, 1972, 1973, 1975, 1977 by the Lockman Foundation. Used by permission.

Interior Illustrations:
Conceptual drawings by Marlin Harris.
Finished illustrations by Ralph Mark Jr.

WestBow Press books may be ordered through booksellers or by contacting:

WestBow Press
A Division of Thomas Nelson & Zondervan
1663 Liberty Drive
Bloomington, IN 47403
www.westbowpress.com
1 (866) 928-1240

ISBN: 978-1-4908-9903-9 (sc)
ISBN: 978-1-4908-9904-6 (e)

Print information available on the last page.

WestBow Press rev. date: 02/04/2016

This book is dedicated to the memory of Peggy Hethcock, whose life epitomized the Beatitudes and touched every person she met with the powerful presence of Jesus Christ living in her.

CONTENTS

FOREWORD

In the opening pages of his book *Let the Beatitudes BE My Attitude in You*, Marlin Harris says that the "Beatitudes are character-building callings from the Master himself to take up a sacred quest to become the person God created you to be." I couldn't agree more.

The Beatitudes have the potential for transforming our lives if we understand the meaning behind Jesus' words. Jesus calls us to love God with all our hearts, souls, and minds, and then, out of that love, serve others. This is a call to a relationship, not just a checklist of dos and don'ts—a relationship with our heavenly Father, who watches over us and desires to live in and through us to touch the lives of hurting people. The Beatitudes remind us we that are blessed, that we will have a deeper joy when we follow his teachings. Allow Marlin to guide you through this rediscovery of a special gift in Scripture, the Beatitudes.

—Wanda S. Lee, National Executive Director, Women's Missionary Union, Southern Baptist Convention; former missionary nurse in St. Vincent, Windward Islands, and author of *The Story Lives On* and *Live the Call*

PREFACE

A Personal Message to the Group Leader

I thank God that through your sensitivity to the prompting of his Holy Spirit you have assumed spiritual leadership to guide this unique study on the Beatitudes. My fervent prayer is that the power of the Beatitudes will be unleashed mightily in your life, in your walk with the Lord, and in the lives of each of your group members. I can bear witness that the Beatitudes have remade my spiritual life, even though beforehand I felt very comfortable and confident with where I was with our Lord. Your group will encounter precious "Beatitude moments" of pure discovery that will open up new dimensions with our Lord and produce a highly charged and overwhelming passion for him. This is what happened to me on a very deep level with each of the Beatitudes. The purpose of this study is to allow God to become greater and even more personal in all our lives, the goal he most longs to accomplish with each of his children.

Jesus desires that his Beatitudes message touch this generation, and you are playing a very important role in helping to make this happen! The Beatitudes have been largely neglected for two thousand years and God wants them to become a dynamic part of who we are as his followers. My desire is that this study will be an unforgettable experience for each person who makes this spiritual pilgrimage! I sincerely admire and appreciate your commitment to lead this dynamic study and group experience.

Below I have listed various resources to make these studies unique and appealing. Before you begin the study, please e-mail me at *marlinharris@hotmail.com* so that once I hear that you will lead the study I will email you my **Dropbox Link** to the folder with all the Beatitude Bible Study Power-Point Presentations for you to use and additional files with information which will be helpful for the Beatitudes Bible Study.

Also I encourage all group members to obtain a copy of *Let the Beatitudes BE My Attitude in You* to use as a personal reference during the study. It will help each person "dig deeper" into each Beatitudes and also be more prepared for each study. Copies of the book are available through the publisher, Westbowpress.com, Amazon.com, Barnesandnoble.com, and also at a discounted price on my website: *questforthebeatitudes.*

org. When ordered from my website I will gladly send each study group member a signed copy of the book.

Study Resources

- Dynamic PowerPoint presentations have been developed to accompany each Beatitudes Bible Study lesson. This is to help facilitate the teaching of each lesson with images and music. These resources provided for the study will lead your group into a full experience of each of the Beatitudes. Each study requires about one hour to complete with your group. This Bible Study Leader Guide has narratives for each slide. Each slide commentary is designated by an individual paragraph or sentence accompanying each slide in the exact order they are presented in the lesson power-points.

- The pivotal point of every lesson is its "Beatitude moment" in which, hopefully, the key message of the Beatitude will be assimilated into each participant's life and walk with our Lord, resulting in a more intense relationship with God.

- Christian contemporary songs cited in the Group Leader Guide are included in the lesson Power-Points to embellish the message of each study. Some are specially included to provide a time of personal reflection about specific life experiences and decisions to be made before our Lord.

- At the conclusion of the Group Leader Guide, you will find a complete listing of songs mentioned in the book and included in the Study. I feel that these songs really help to magnify the message and personal experience within each lesson. Just for your reference, you will find on the Beatitudes website YouTube links for all songs available through that resource. On one of the final pages of this Leader Guide is a listing of all songs with their YouTube links. Notation is made if the song is not available on YouTube. This is strictly for your reference. All songs and music videos are already inserted into the Power-Point Presentations.

- Selected music videos from *The Story* will also powerfully bring home the main messages of different studies. These are also included in the Power-Point presentations. I suggest obtaining a copy of *The Story* DVD in order to use other music videos from this album for other studies or messages. A link to purchase *The Story* DVD is also on the website.

- Additional unique group activities are also incorporated into different studies to emphasize on a personal level the messages revealed in each of the Beatitudes.

- There are suggestions for weekly "BEing in the Beatitudes" activities to be done between the weekly group sessions so that members can devote themselves to further study and reflection regarding that week's Beatitude message.

- *"The Beatitudes Life"* album. God inspired to me the writing and arrangement of a special song about each of the Beatitudes, along with a "Beginning" and "Conclusion" song. These songs will be compelling for your group to listen to and sing along with at the conclusion of each study. Each song is included at the end of each Beatitude lesson Power-Point. This album is also available on the website *questforthebeatitudes.org*.

- An additional resource to share with each group member who is utilizing the book, *"Let the Beatitudes Be My Attitude in You"* is *The Participant Guide* which was developed by Ray Cureton, a close friend and pastor, who voluntarily designed this guide to assist readers of the book to identify the key ideas presented. It was not possible to include every element of the book in the Bible Study and *The Participant Guide* will help each reader delve deeper into the material of the book and come to the Beatitudes Study very well prepared to capture the strong message of each lesson. I have included a copy of *The Participant Guide* at the end of this Group Leader Guide with answers to all the questions, in case you wish to discuss any of these in the study or some members need the answers to specific questions in *The Participant Guide.* Here is Ray's biography;

  Dr. Ray H. Cureton is a Presbyterian Church in America ordained minister with 17 years pastoral ministry experience. Dr. Cureton also retired from the USAF after 20 years where he served as a Security Policeman and an Air Force Recruiter. Dr. Cureton received a Bachelor of Arts degree (1984), a Master of Divinity (1998), and a Doctor of Ministry in Pastoral Leadership (2012) from Columbia International University, Columbia, SC. He is married to the former Silvana S. DiPaolo of Paris France. The Curetons have 2 children and 7 grandchildren.

Thank you again so much for assuming the responsibility to lead this very significant spiritual study for your group members. Please feel free to contact me at the e-mail address mentioned above with any comments, suggestions, or ideas. This study will be enhanced with your valuable feedback.

After the conclusion of the study, I would welcome input from you and any members of your group concerning their most memorable experiences, testimonials, and any suggestions to improve this study for future groups.

May the Lord greatly bless, inspire, and lead you in every moment of each study. Please contact me before beginning the study, and I will covet with you to pray fervently each day for an authentic and unforgettable Beatitude experience for you and your group.

Most sincerely in Christ,
Marlin

ACKNOWLEDGMENTS

After publication of the book *Let the Beatitudes BE My Attitude in You,* I shared copies with pastors, lay leaders, and spiritually minded comrades in the kingdom of God. I was invited to share copies with colleagues at the high school where I teach. There was a very strong response for numerous copies of the book.

Shortly after, I had the privilege of placing the book in the hands of interested readers, Barry Barnett, director of the online teaching program in which I am involved, who informed me that he was using the book to introduce the Beatitudes to his Sunday school class of junior high students. A few weeks later, Pam Frederick, a dedicated Christian and administrator at my high school, said she felt led to conduct a study on the Beatitudes with her Wednesday night Bible study group. Most pleased and somewhat surprised that the book was twice being used to guide a group study, I offered to come and share introductory ideas on the Scripture passage and a personal testimony of how the Beatitudes had deepened my life with the Lord.

That evening was a very emotional experience as the Lord prepared hearts to encounter each of the Beatitudes on a very profound level. I left this session convinced that a group setting could be one of the most powerful ways to experience the Beatitudes and that God was behind this strategy. I wanted to help Pam by developing a leader guide booklet and PowerPoints for each session. Each week she told me about the Beatitude moment with her group. Since that time, other study groups have begun, across our country, further assuring me that this strategy is definitively of God and will be an effective tool to carry the Beatitudes message to this generation.

Another hero in this process has been my twin brother, Donovan Harris, who has dedicated significant time and energy to design the cover, share ideas, and prepare graphic files for the production process. He has contributed greatly to making this leader guide a reality.

I am so thankful to Barry, Pam, Donovan, and others who have inspired and assisted in the development of this guide and the additional resources that I pray will bring the blessings of the Beatitudes through a very personal experience to many of our generation.

LESSON 1

Introduction

Before preaching The Sermon on the Mount, Jesus summoned his disciples to the top of the Mount and he carefully shared the Beatitudes with them. After presenting each Beatitude to them Jesus declared that they would make his followers the salt and light of this world. The Beatitudes will help us flavor the world around us with his love and goodness and perpetually shine his holy light on others. The Beatitudes were not only for his original disciples, but for every one of his followers. Jesus is eagerly waiting to take your hand and lead you into the Beatitudes Quest so that they will become an integral part of your life and walk with him. Seize Our Savior's hand and enter into the spiritual riches of the Beatitudes that Jesus has prepared for you.

The Beatitudes are God's beauty in us. Let his beauty shine through you!

"Beatitudes" is an unusual word and relatively unknown. Think of it as Be-attitudes. God wants his attitude to "be" in us. Allowing the Beatitudes to shine through us is dependent upon our personal attitude. Ask group members, *"What is an attitude? How is it formed?"*

1. Our attitudes are produced via a process.
2. This process begins with our thoughts. From where do our thoughts originate? With what do we fill our minds?
3. Our thoughts lead us to actions. We act according to our thoughts.
4. Our pattern of outward actions and words from our inner selves manifest our behavior.
5. Would you agree that our attitude basically defines who we are and how we act?
6. What other factors can determine our attitude? Is it more outward circumstances or inward determination?

7. Should our attitude be up and down or consistent?

8. Do you know someone with "an attitude"? Is the idea behind this phrase positive or negative? What is the behavior pattern of this type of person? (These answers will probably be fairly negative.)

9. Ask, "How would you describe your own prevalent attitude(s)? Could it/they be improved? Would such improvement make you a better and happier person?

10. Our genuine attitude is found within ourselves and is who we are on the inside. Our Lord longs to influence our attitude. He wants us to possess his Beatitudes so that his attitude can be in us! The Beatitudes bring abundant blessings and promises from Above. Let's look at the attitudes that God wants in us.

Now have the group read together the Beatitudes (Matthew 5:3-10) as listed on the next two slides. After reading through this passage request any comments or observations about these verses. Perhaps some will mention that parts are difficult to understand with human logic and challenging to apply to life in today's world. Assure them that the Beatitudes are actually very practical in God's Kingdom and will change their hearts to be more like his.

Unfortunately, the Beatitudes have lain ignored and unexplored for centuries by Christendom. Why would that be? They are precious spiritual treasures from Jesus, stored up for us with great blessings for every believer.

The Beatitudes will by no means make us perfect, but they will bring us so much closer to God!

And him closer to us.

What is Jesus' deep desire for us? (*To find profound happiness, contentment, fulfillment and confidence in our walk with him.*)

What is true blessedness on this earth? (*Being one with God and seizing his victorious attitude in this life.*)

The Beatitudes relate strongly to the two "greatest commandments," found in Matthew 22:35-40. "A Pharisee named Nicodemus came to Jesus late one evening and asked: "Teacher, which is the greatest commandment in the law?" Jesus replied, "You shall love the Lord your God with all your heart and with all your soul and with all your mind. This is the first and greatest commandment. And the second is like it: Love your neighbor as yourself. All the law and the prophets hang on these two commandments."

A. **What is the basic idea in both of these commandments?** Both of these commands deal with relationships—first and most important is our relationship with God, and second, our relationship with one another, especially those we can't stand or those who can't stand us. Let's look in more detail at each of these relationships.

B. **Our relationship with God.** He is to be *número uno* in our hearts, souls, and minds. Our personal relationship with God is critical and fundamental. We are to love him with the totality of who we are. Help the group define the differences between heart, soul, and mind. The *heart* is the seat of our emotions, values, motivations, and intentions, even to the innermost recesses of our being. Our *soul* is that eternal part of us that Jesus died to save and who we will be when our ordained days have been completed here on earth. Our *mind* is not only the sum of all the knowledge and experiences acquired in life, but also the great gift of intelligence that instantly processes this information for useful purposes. How should we process what is going on around us? God's desire is that we process it with heavenly wisdom, thinking and acting to glorify him and benefit all involved.

Our passion for God must originate from these three elemental dimensions of our being: our heart, our soul, our mind—the sum of who we are, aside from our physical bodies. When we eliminate these three elements, what is left? Not much, only a lifeless physical body. We are to love God with everything there is within us!

C. **Our relationship with others.** We are to love them with God's unconditional love. This commandment can grate against our human nature, because our normal human desire is to put ourselves in first place. But Jesus and God's Word require us to consider others first, even to the radical extreme of loving our enemies, those who wish to do us evil. Only when we love God to the extent required in the first commandment do we become capable of achieving the second commandment. We cannot do it on our own!

D. **The Beatitudes enable us to live out the two greatest commandments.** The first four Beatitudes focus on intensifying our relationship with God and allowing him to fully occupy our lives. The second four activate his essential attributes in our lives so that we will love our neighbor as ourselves. Our mind-set and values are elevated through the Beatitudes to discover a love for God so deep that it floods our heart, soul, and mind and then extends beyond us to all those around us.

The Beatitudes assure that we will "keep increasing," just as Jesus did on earth. Luke 2:52 says, "And Jesus kept increasing in wisdom and in stature, and in favor with God and man." This is what the Beatitudes will do for us. They will keep increasing us in wisdom, in spiritual stature, and in favor with God and man. Our favor is not earned, but is a consuming love for God that allows us to be his instrument on earth! It is a continual process of "BEcoming" for him.

The Beatitudes Are All about Who we are TO BE for God. Letting God "BE" in us. "Being" leads to "doing" for him. (Ask, "Which is more important- who we are what or we do? Doesn't "being" lead to "doing"?)

A. **BEing in full fellowship with him.** The Beatitudes help you discover the depth of relationship that God originally had with man in the Garden of Eden. That is the level of fellowship that he desires to enjoy with every one of us.

B. **BEcoming who he created you to be.** God created each of us with a specific purpose for our lives. What amazing blessings we will miss if we don't find that divine path for our lives! God's kingdom will lack the impact that He intends for each of us to have on it.

C. **BEing totally spiritually sensitive to all that God is doing in your life!.** Daily occurrences will suddenly have more significance as we become aware that every incident in our daily path has a purpose from the Lord. We may not understand the meaning immediately, but he will reveal it to us in his perfect timing. His spiritual radar will become active within us, providing specific feelings of guidance that we know we are to follow. Then we will see how he has placed us in a position to be used by him!

D. **BEing an effective instrument for His Kingdom on earth!** The Beatitudes will lead us to do exactly what he wants us to do. Don't wait for others to do something that God wants you to do. We are never too young to be used by God. Commit to let God use you now. Just imagine what God can do through you over the length of your life. Billy Graham began preaching when he was fourteen. Consider Samuel and David in the Bible and the work that God began in their young lives.

Offer a challenge: If you want to discover the plan that God has for your life the Beatitudes will carry you there!

E. BEcoming more beautiful before him and others. The Beatitudes are precious jewels in God's Word. We are about to pick them up, carefully examine each one, polish them up, and use them to adorn ourselves before him. Talk about how jewelry and scarves are popular in fashion and how they enhance our appearance before others—they keep us from looking plain. That's how the Beatitudes will affect our relationship with our Lord and with all those around us. They are God's jewelry and will make us more beautiful, transforming us into sensitive, active, and useful servants for him in this world!

When we become the "who" God desires, we will richly experience each blessing and promise enumerated in the Beatitudes. We encounter *makarios* blessings, the inner and deep contentment evident of pure character and motivation, not subject to outward circumstances. God is fully alive and active within us!

Let's leave the Land of Lukewarmness Read Revelation 3:15-16, which says, "I know your deeds, that you are neither hot nor cold. I wish you were either one or the other! So, because you are lukewarm— neither hot nor cold—I am about to spit you out of my mouth." We can easily slip into a lukewarm complacency concerning our Lord, and his strong language here unmistakably illustrates his extreme disgust with such an attitude. Is this a problem with some churches today? We must leave the Land of Lukewarmness and take up the quest for the Beatitudes today! We must become more passionate about our relationship with God and about what he means to us.

Enter the Land of the Beatitudes, a remarkable spiritual journey that is awaiting you. Each drawing represents the essence of that particular Beatitude which we will experience intensely and intimately one at a time. This spiritual quest will transport you to never-imagined depths in your relationships with God and with others.

The Beatitudes are an exciting adventure of pure discovery about God and about you. The Beatitudes are a God given gauntlet he placed before each believer. Pick it up to encounter "pure discovery" about God and about yourself. You will also surrender a part of your heart to God in each of the Beatitudes. In the end, you will be remade and will come to know God heart to heart. This won't happen unless you are prepared to hand over to him a piece of your heart in each Beatitude. Be ready to experience a serious Beatitude moment within each one! The experience will become a great spiritual enabler in your life.

Through this study you will now begin the Beatitudes Quest that Our Lord desires for every believer!

Play "Your Heart" by Chris Tomlin, a music video from *The Story*. After viewing the video, ask the group how many want to experience the message of this song—to have a heart like God's heart—because that's what the Beatitudes desire to do for every believer.

Let's begin the Beatitudes Quest! They will lead us to have a heart like God's heart. Jesus will become more alive in each of us! And we will become more like him!

They will prompt us to carry the precious Beatitudes message to our generation.

Play the concluding song for the Introductory lesson from The Beatitudes Life album: ***"Treasures from Jesus—the Beatitudes."*** Tell the group to imagine that they are hearing a group of young angels singing about these spiritual treasures created by Jesus for each of us.

Final comment: The Beatitudes truly represent Jesus' character and personality on earth, and all his Godly attributes that blessed everyone he met, and all of us today with the eternal gift of salvation.

Map of the Land of the Beatitudes

The Rich Ridge
Of Righteousness

The Mirrored Mountains
Of Meekness

The Marshlands
Of Mourning

Enter By The Cross
Of the Poor in Heart

The Land of

CONCEPTUAL DRAWINGS: MARLIN J. HARRIS /
FINAL ILLUSTRATIONS: RALPH A. MARK, JR.

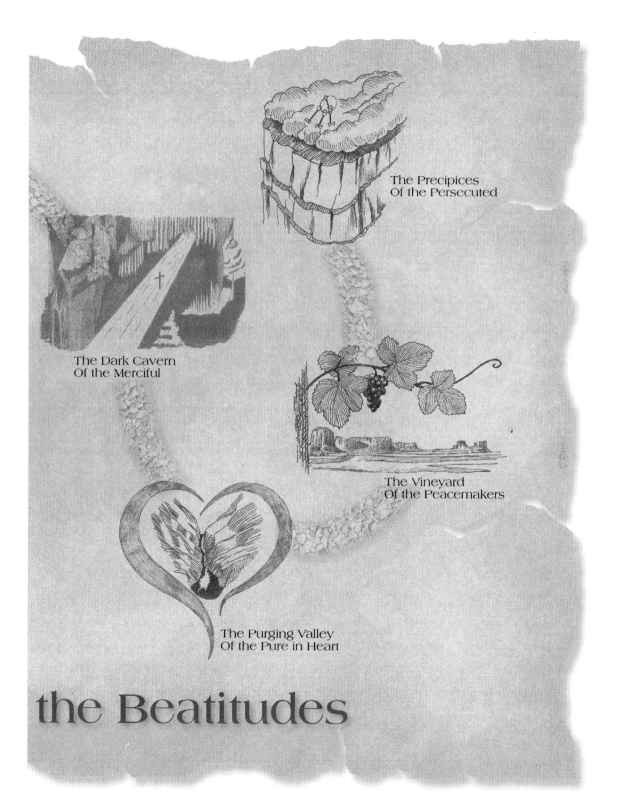

The Precipices
Of the Persecuted

The Dark Cavern
Of the Merciful

The Vineyard
Of the Peacemakers

The Purging Valley
Of the Pure in Heart

the Beatitudes

Blessed are the poor in spirit, for theirs is the kingdom of God (Matthew 5:3)

Introductory remarks: Although we now are much more aware of all that the Beatitudes promise for us, we have not yet begun the Quest. We are still on the outside, peering in. How do we enter and begin our journey?

Show the Lesson 1 slide with the first Beatitude. We will plunge in to the *"poor in spirit"*. What does it mean? Does it not seem the opposite of how we imagine ourselves to be in the Kingdom of God---*rich in spirit*? But to enter the Land of the Beatitudes we have to get outside our own perception of our personal spiritual status. First we must consider the following:

The Grandeur of God!

How do you consider yourself before God? Pretty satisfied, with ample "brownie points," and a confident understanding of him. That's the way I saw myself for many years; however, in the first Beatitude, we discover our true position before God.

Imagine being outside at night to view the awe inspiring heavens and the stars. Can you count them? Is this all of them? No. We are able to see only a very small part of the universe, but that tiny portion alone is amazing. God created all of this and so much more.

There are millions of solar systems in the universe, yet God is interested in our minuscule planet. God constantly surveys his infinite creation. He is involved in all of it.

How many people call this planet home? Almost seven billion people live on earth. God is interested in all those who have lived on earth, all those now alive, and all who will live here in the future. How incredible is that?

Our God, the Creator of the infinite universe, is interested in you, one of seven billion inhabitants of the earth. Each of us is an insignificant speck on this planet, which is a mere speck in the Milky Way, which is only a speck in the universe. We are each a speck reduced infinitely three times!

Show group members the YouTube video, *The Detail of the Universe-This will blow your mind,* which is acompnanied with two songs from Kutless, *"God of Wonders"* and *"Amazed".* This video first conveys the infinite depths of the universe and then, God's intricate design within us. The video zooms from Earth to the perceived limits of the universe, and then returns all the way down to the smallest measurable particle within his created entities. This will give the group unbelievable insight into God's immeasurable creation and unimaginably intricate design within each of us.

Now comment that we are totally insignificant compared with the grandeur of God, yet he is interested in us! This is unbelievably humbling!

Present these comparisons between God and humanity: (the slide will show the characteristics of God first, then each comparison with man beside it.

God is forever; our days are numbered.

He is present in the entire universe; we are confined to a single place and time.

His knowledge is inexhaustible; ours is limited.

He creates into being with the spoken word; we strive to fashion with our minds and our hands.

His will is permanent and purposeful; ours is fickle and floundering.

His character is pure and holy; we are corrupted with sin.

His love is unconditional; ours is selfish and reciprocal.

His mercy forgives and forgets; ours is self-serving with a memory.

God is so far beyond us, and yet our Creator seeks his lost creation. (See Beatitudes book, page 17.)

Who Are the Poor in Spirit?

(Picture of cardboard sign) The poor in spirit realize who they are before God. We are not just poor, spiritually, but in reality we are destitute beggars before God. We cannot approach God strictly on our own. Read or have a group member read this commentary from John Gill. (See Beatitudes book, page 15.)

> All mankind are spiritually poor; they have nothing to eat that is fit or proper; nor any clothes to wear, but rags; nor are they able to purchase either; they have no money to buy with; they are in debt, owe ten thousand talents, and have nothing with which to pay it! They are in such a condition, that they are not able to help themselves. Most of mankind are insensible that this is their condition, but think themselves rich. Human nature yearns to play a part in salvation by weighing good deeds against the bad to earn our entry to Heaven. "There is a way that seems right to man, but in the end it leads to death" (Proverbs 14:12). But there is "none righteous, no not one" (Romans 3:10).
>
> Those who can see their spiritual poverty and want, freely acknowledge it, bewail it, and mourn over it. They are humbled for it and broken under a sense of it . . . and frankly acknowledge that all they have, or hope to have, is owing to the free grace of God. Now these are the persons intended in this place, and that is why they are called blessed.

The poor in spirit approach our God with quiet and confident desperation. In *John's Story: The Last Eyewitness*, the apostle states, "We face the ugliness of our own humanity. I cannot stand to be alone in my own presence for another instant! We must feel that God has thrust a lantern into our inner self and searched us for every weakness, frailty, and sin. We must face the ugliness of our own humanity and be brought to tears."

Play "Face Down" by Casting Crowns and ask each member to listen carefully and seriously reflect upon the message of this song. (Proceed to next slide to begin the song)

Now recognize all that God is and all that we aren't! What of value you can give God? He gave you life, he gave you your body, which is unbelievably intricate in all its workings, and he gave you your mind, talent, intellect, and eternal soul. Everything you are came from God, and your eternity belongs to God.

Enter the Land of the Beatitudes by the cross of Christ.")

Ask: What can save us before God? Our beloved "brownie points" don't mean a blessed thing! Nor do our insignificant selves. Only Jesus Christ's personal sacrifice for each of us on the cross of Calvary can bring us before God. Jesus said, "I am the way, the truth, and the life: no one comes to the Father, but through me" (John 14:6). To enter the Land of the Beatitudes, we must sacrifice our spiritual pride and admit our total spiritual worthlessness. We must throw aside any prideful accomplishments and/or feelings of spiritual self-sufficiency.

We Enter the Land of the Beatitudes with Only the Cross of Christ

Jesus said, "Take up my cross and follow me daily." His precious cross is our lone spiritual asset, our only means of entering the Land of the Beatitudes. Our life of sin and without God is now all in the past.

Play "Yesterday Is Gone" by Charlie Hall from his album *The Rising*. (Audio embedded on this slide)

"Yesterday is gone, You've forgiven all my wrongs, and filled my heart with songs. I'm chasing after your heart!"

The Beatitude Moment for the Poor in Spirit

What two realities must we grasp in this first Beatitude? First, we must acknowledge God's vast greatness and, secondly, comprehend our impoverished spiritual state. Here, during a time of silent prayer, 1) ask group members to recount when they became conscious of their own spiritual poverty and the need of Jesus in their life. But after this critical moment we are easily tempted to begin accumulating our own strong spiritual pride.

Now place before Christ any undue spiritual pride of which the Holy Spirit convicts you and passionately take up the cross of Christ which paid the price of your sin, in order to enter the Land of the Beatitudes. If you have a cross standing upright in the room, and as group members pray ask they to write personal statements admitting to God that they have no spiritual accomplishments to claim before him, only the salvation he has given them. They will sign their statements where they are or pin or tape them to the cross, and then bow down by the cross and pray to Jesus, thanking him for giving eternal life promise to carry his cross daily.

Conclude the Beatitude moment by saying, "We are beggars who have found the glorious splendor of our King. Our admission of spiritual poverty enables him to make us rich. He is the eternal oasis in our spiritual desert. God's desire is not to lord it over us, but to know us thoroughly through a deep and loving relationship. He yearns to embrace us with his love and to make us the very best we can be. What a Lord and Savior!

Understanding our spiritual poverty before God is the passageway into the land of spiritual growth. Spiritual poverty produces spiritual riches that we can relish every day here on earth and throughout eternity. James 4:10 exclaims, "Humble yourselves in the presence of the Lord and He will exalt you."

The poor in spirit are blessed to experience heaven on earth. Theirs is the kingdom of heaven whether here or there. They desperately seek God because they know that they desperately need God.

A Daily Encounter with God

Beginning each day with God is vital for the *poor in spirit*. You must commit to him the day and plead for his Spirit to invade you and dwell in you, enabling you to live above any circumstances awaiting you. This is also the time to pray for Jesus to reveal to you even more the extent of your poverty and his wondrous greatness. He will become the boundless generator in your life. You will submit to his holy governance your thoughts, words, actions, and reactions as you place the day in his loving hands.

Thoughts and Meditations

Each day this week in your time with the Lord, ask him:

- How will you amaze me today? Wait for his answers—they will astound you and be totally different each day.
- Reflect upon a recent experience in which God redeemed or rescued you, and thank him for it.

Closing Prayer

(Gather is a circle with all holding hands.)

Lord, reveal my true spiritual poverty and your great majesties and riches for me. Lead me into an ever richer and more sincere relationship with you, my Savior and Lord. Help me to become the "who" you want me to be. Amen.

Forget your past…

Beatitudes song: ***"The Splendor of My King" sung by Bucky Heard***

Final Comment: The great Southern Baptist preacher, Vance Havner, once said, "Humility is not thinking meanly (or badly) of oneself, but rather it means not thinking of yourself at all. "Isn't this what being poor in spirit is as well—the ability to so understand our own spiritual poverty that we look only at the majesty and glory of God to find true significance in life rather than at ourselves and our own accomplishments?

Conclusion

Jesus has come so far to find you, to save you, and to bring you to and through the door of the first Beatitude. Here the poor in spirit bow in brokenness to comprehend God's great reality and the richness of his kingdom. Consider yourself now a spiritual knight, equipped with a light within and ready to begin your quest for the remaining Beatitudes. Prepare yourself for quite a journey!

BEing the Beatitudes

Memorize the first Beatitude and read and reflect daily upon the Scripture verses listed at the end of chapter 2 in the book and decide which one speaks most meaningfully to you. (Copies of these verses are also included at the end of the study and should be distributed to participants to use in their daily reflections if they do not have a copy of the book.)

Blessed are those who mourn, for they shall be comforted (Matthew 5:4)

Read the Beatitude together with the group. Then comment that this Beatitude is about a lot more, than just being "comforted." You will experience much more than this!

View *The Story* music video "*Who but You*" by Mark Hall and Megan Garrett about the life of Abraham. (Start the video on the next slide)

Abraham's Beatitude Moment

(Slide with Abraham climbing Mount Moriah) Give the following background:

Remind the group that Abraham was now 90 years old and with his son that had been promised to him by God twenty years ago one night as he gazed into the heavens.

God had promised him that the seed of his future generations would be as numerous as the stars he was looking at spread across the sky.

- Ask: What could Abraham have been thinking as he climbed Mount Moriah with Isaac? Very puzzled and confused: Why does God want my only son that he has given me? How will my descendants become as numerous as the stars in the sky if my firstborn is sacrificed? But I will only obey him, as I have done from my first step out of the Land of Ur decades ago.
- Slide with Abraham about to sacrifice Isaac
- Imagine Abraham's dread transformed to elation when God cried out his name as he was about to plunge a knife into Isaac's heart.
- Slide with "Dream Your dream in me"

- What was the message of the music video about Abraham? (*Lord, dream your dream in me!*)
- What can keep God from dreaming his dream in us? Due to some tragic circumstances surrounding us or the deep bereavement within us.

When Sorrow Strikes Like a Tsunami

Ask group members to silently reflect upon any tragedy or great sadness that has occurred in their lives.

It could have been the loss of a loved one, the departure of a close friend, Regret and remorse from a divorce experience or disappointment in how someone has treated them.

Mourning from anger or bitterness from a difficult situation.

Ask, "Are you mourning today?" Then share the following:

When sorrow strikes us like a tsunami, leaving only grief and despair, that is when we discover the truth about our relationship with God—or more accurately, his relationship with us. In these moments of desolation and desperation, when we are totally absorbed in our grief, God comes to find us. How do we respond? Do we let him in to minister to our heart or do we decide to wallow in self-pity, anger, and bitterness?

Play "*Carry Me to the Cross*" by Kutless. (Begin video song on the next slide)

When we are dealing with the death of a loved one, God desires to fill us with an overwhelming sense of peace that surpasses all understanding. (See Philippians 4:6-8—written on slide.) God is with us in the darkest moments of our pilgrimage on earth. What other faith or religion offers such consolation?

Mourning equals a broken heart--that God desires to mend. There are many situations which can make us mourn. How are we handling them? Do we hold resentment, have negative feelings about ourselves, or harbor anger at God or someone else? Discuss these types of mourning with the group, and then conclude this conversation by asking whether this is the way God wants us to handle these problems?

God Is Offering His Insurmountable Peace and Comfort to You!

Our God is with us, whatever the problem we face. He wants us to turn it over to him. Our dependence on him must be as solid as stone. We must trust God to carry this difficulty for us and handle it according to his perfect will. Psalm 56:8 says, "Thou has taken account of my wandering, and put my tears in thy bottle." God stores up every tear you have ever cried. He treasures you that much! Despite your problems, his plan for you will be only for your best. He promises that your mourning will be met with incomparable comfort from above. He wishes to carry these burdens for you, to free you from them. In the first Beatitude, we began to discover the grandeur and greatness of God. How can you not release your problems to a God like that!

The Marshlands of Mourning

Discuss the illustration "The Marshlands of Mourning" from the Land of the Beatitudes map, which depicts Jesus reaching down from his heavenly home to rescue us from the Marshlands of Mourning, the burdens weighing us down.

Jesus is our rock, no matter how strong the waves are against us. He is our source of greatest comfort and consolation that begins when we call on God. He will strengthen, teach, encourage, and exhort us and reveal where we have gone wrong to give us wisdom and to make us better people. Our Lord looks to the future, not to the past. Jesus gives us a future and a hope!

Jesus Christ is our consolation experience! Rivers of living water flow out of Christ's heart. "Whoever believes in me, rivers of living water will flow from within them" (John 7:38). As Jesus said to the Samaritan woman at the well, "Everyone who drinks this water will be thirsty again, but whoever drinks the water I give them will never thirst. Indeed, the water I give them will become in them a spring of water welling up to eternal life" (John 4:13-14).

Jesus is the Wellspring of our life. He is our Well and He will make us well!

The Beatitude Moment for Those Who Mourn

Ask members of the group to think about the burdens that they are carrying and that need to be released and given to God. This is the moment to release their troubles to Jesus rather than continuing to carry them on their own.

As they listen to "The Well" by Casting Crowns request group members to reflect on the burdens that they need to release to Our Lord. (The video song is on the next slide)

Why did God never answer the "why's" that Job continuously questioned him? Because God came down to be with him. We must release the "why's" of our sufferings to God. Don't be a "why-ner" before God. You have given him your burdens. Release your sufferings with a total affirmation of God's power, peace, and love for you.

What was our mourning is now a new morning! Only the living water of Christ in our distressed and parched hearts can provide the renewing consolation that restores our souls from the physical, emotional, or spiritual mourning we are experiencing. We must ask him to flood us! Christ promises water that is never-ending, spiritually powerful, and totally filling. Jesus is the water from the well. He is the crystal-clear water coursing through us to carry away our sorrows and burdens. "My peace I give to you," he promises in John 14:27. After we have tasted him, nothing else can console us. Our mourning is converted to peace and joy.

Reach out to the mourning. When we conquer our mourning we can minister to others as Jesus works through us.

We can offer his unsurpassed comfort to them which will make an incredible difference in their lives.

The God who cares for us began drawing us to him in the first Beatitude. Now Jesus carries us to the second Beatitude to encounter his incomparable consolation. Such comfort leads to peace and to a total dependence upon God in all his ways and in his timing. His ways are perfect.

Our God is the God of Comfort. . Mourning must result in totally turning our burdens over to God with sincere faith that he will carry us through whatever valleys we are experiencing. We are freed from worrying and wringing our hands when things don't go exactly as we planned or anticipated. Waiting on God to work his will in our lives is a liberating experience that cultivates patience, dependence, and faith, and elevates us to a new level of life and living.

Our Tapestry of Life

A man arrived in heaven and began to question the many trials and tribulations he had confronted in life on earth. The Lord pulled out a thready, unkempt piece of cloth to show the man. It looked so tangled and disarrayed that he gasped at its appearance.

Then Jesus turned it over to display a lovely, intricately designed tapestry and commented to the man, "What you were seeing was the underside, but God was weaving a beautiful and powerful story with your life."

Show the next two slides with beautiful tapestry designs

Many times, we as mourners can see only the underside in this life. We must trust the true pattern that the Master is weaving with our lives and submit our threads to him each day. Our mourning will produce a majestic tapestry for his purposes. The Beatitude for mourners grants freedom from the worry, want, and care of each day and enables them to live above life's circumstances. We must not be sucked into the emotional roller coaster of life where Satan delights in placing us! In this Beatitude, we discover the joy of complete dependence on God's comfort and absolute relief from daily cares and burdens as we turn them over to him. We must return from whatever crises we are experiencing. We must let God dream his dream in us!

"God uses the difficult circumstances in life to purify us as a refining fire. Lord, please work in my life to make me purely dependent upon you" (T. W. Hunt and Claude N. King, *The Mind of Christ*).

Thoughts for Meditation

- What is breaking my heart today? Give it to God.
- What is breaking God's heart today? Be used by God to help resolve it.

Our God provides, and we must depend solely upon him! Blessed are those who mourn, for they find a whole new morning and rely upon God in a whole new way!

Play "You're Everything I Need" by Kutless. (Music video is on the next slide)

Jesus is everything we need. Give all your cares to him. The message of this Beatitude, Totally depend upon God.

Forget your past …

Play the concluding Beatitude song, *"My Heart Will Break No More" sung by Annette Herndon*

Closing Prayer for Comfort Taken from 2 Corinthians 1:3-4

(Gather in a circle with all holding hands.)

"Praise be to the God and Father of our Lord Jesus Christ, the Father of compassion and the God of all comfort, who comforts us in all our troubles, so that we can comfort those in any trouble with the comfort we ourselves receive from God." Amen.

Final comment: How does this Beatitude strongly apply to our spiritual journey on earth?

BEing the Beatitudes

Memorize this Beatitude and review the first one. Reflect daily on the Scripture verses for this chapter.

Blessed are the meek, for they shall inherit the earth (Matthew 5:5)

Have the group read together the Beatitude on meekness.

Consider how far we have come in our Beatitudes quest.

We have crucified our spiritual pride and magnified the majesty of our God

We have come to the Well and released all our burdens to Jesus.

We have eliminated two major distractions that detour many from God. There is still one other serious contender.

What are the most popular electronic devices in modern society? How do they impact us?

(Next slide) Show the group these numerous scenarios so common in our society today—iPhones, iPods, and iPads everywhere. These amazing instruments keep us connected to family and friends, but in reality what has become our emphasis in using them?

People are supposedly socializing. They are occupying space together, but how much socializing is actually going on? Each is in his or her own world with their i-Device.

Our society is clearly the "i-Generation". Albert Einstein said, decades before social media was even conceived, "I fear the day that technology will surpass our human interaction. The world will have a generation of idiots."

What is their primary purpose? Who is usually the star of the show? Many times it is the person holding them and manipulating them. The purpose of the "I" technology and social media is to link us together. But, in reality, is that the true result? Are we the "I" generation or the "ME" generation?

It easily becomes all about "me". The first two Beatitudes teach us that we are not paramount. God is much more important and wants to care for us. The Beatitude of meekness elevates this message to a much higher level.

Meekness is all about ridding ourselves of the "mighty me" that easily demands control of our lives.

Ask the group: How would you define meekness? After receiving answers comment that "meekness" is an ancient word, and some probably do not know its meaning. Although the first two letters of the word are "m-e" meekness requires much less of me andmuch more of God. This is in contrast to the world today which is mostlyall about "me".

Two good definitions of *meekness* are "absolute strength under perfect control" or "strength in gentleness." Ask the group: Does the lion control the lamb or the lamb control the lion? In true meekness, the lamb must be in control.

Living a "Turn the Cheek" Mentality

Jesus tells us that "whoever slaps you on the right cheek, turn to him the other also" (Matthew 5:39). Is this a natural reaction? What exactly does this mean?

Does it mean that you are to let people brutalize you, and not put up a fight?

No, Jesus is saying that whatever you are doing or wherever you are headed in the kingdom of God, don't be detoured, distracted, or deterred from it. Keep on keeping on, regardless of what happens. Let God work out his purpose in you. Don't be prevented from achieving his purpose in your life and dream his dream in you!

To achieve this goal, you must keep your "me" in check. You have to put yourself in the back seat and not let your "me" drive your emotions! That's not easy. Christ must be in charge for this to happen. Another excellent definition of *meekness* is "weakness does not define meekness."

This requires more of him and less of you. The gentleness of Jesus must control you! As we look back on Jesus' time here on earth, this is exactly how he lived his thirty-three years—steadily and strategically stepping forward each day toward his goal of redemption for the world. Every step, every decision, every word was made in service of this grand, eternal, and all-inclusive goal. His meekness permitted him to achieve the result that he had resolved to accomplish and permitted us to be able to inherit his offer of salvation to us.

Claim the Mirrored Mountains of Meekness

In the center of the Land of the Beatitudes stand the Mirrored Mountains. You acquire meekness in the ascent to the top. At this summit, you must submit yourself ever more to Jesus so that he will become more visible in you and be clearly seen in your reflection.

Why are these mountains mirrored?

Because they reflect whatever image is before them.

We must reflect the "Great I Am" light that Jesus desires to shine through us.

Optional: Do reading from *The Powerful Pilgrimage of a Suffering Saint (concluding novel in book).* Let three group members read this dramatically and with feeling; it would be best if they have rehearsed the reading. Parts are: Jesus, Wesley, Narrator

SCRIPT FOR "THE MIRRORED MOUNTAINS OF MEEKNESS" READING (Separate file in Dropbox)

Jesus: "Wesley, you have a difficult task ahead of you," Jesus said. "You must forget yourself—your selfish ambitions, your self-seeking motives, your self-centered attitude, all of which are products of the sinful pride in your life. We will deal with that deep-seated pride later, but for now you must learn to let "self" take a back seat. This is what meekness means, my brother, meekness is all about going on, and that's what you're about to do for me. You are going to negotiate this slippery, mirrored mountain to its summit. This exercise will be a doubly difficult because you will see your reflection with each step. Youe "self" will be constantly looking back at you, demanding your attention and revealing your every emotion and reaction. As difficult as it will be, this climb will take you to higher heights with me. And when you reach the summit, your reflection will change. Instead of your face, you will begin to see mine."

Narrator: Wes was puzzled, but more than ready to begin the climb. Seeing his face at every step and turn was an uncomfortable experience, and the mountain was steeper than it had appeared below. Each step became increasingly difficult as the ledge supporting him narrowed with every foot of ascent. His reflection showed his mounting fear.

Wesley: "My 'me' is too big, because that's all I'm seeing," he thought. "Where's Jesus in me? I don't see him at all!"

Narrator: At that precise moment, he noticed a slight flicker in the glass. A verse came to mind.

Wesley: "Now we see through a glass darkly..."

Narrator: That was certainly what he was experiencing, just a dark glass with his own anxious face peering back. The glass glimmered again, and Wes saw gentle eyes gazing lovingly back at him as he clung to the mountain face. He couldn't look down—it was too frightening and paralyzing, but he couldn't stop climbing—he was only halfway up. Gradually, he began to feel the ability to let himself go and let Jesus become more visible in the reflective glass.

Wesley: "This is what I must do to make it to the top!"

Narrator: The kind eyes reflected back more clearly, and then a radiant smile appeared, encouraging him to press upward. With only the smallest ledge supporting him now, focusing was extremely hard. But to reach the summit, he knew his mind had to be absolutely on Christ. Only Christ could control each careful movement upward. And with each supreme effort, both physical and mental, Jesus' face became more evident, giving to Wes the strength and determination to make it to the top. Fear was gone, replaced by the sole desire to let Christ become as much of him as possible. With one last push, Wes made it! And the face of Christ was no longer a reflection but a reality, as Jesus stood there smiling down at him. Wes joyfully thought of the rest of the verse—

Wesley: "then we shall see him face to face, in total light." "My Lord and my God!" (kneels at Jesus' feet)

Jesus: "Yes, Wesley. I came to save you, which is as far as many of my followers ever decide to travel with me, I died to also be their Lord, a generous and loving Lord, to bring them into the fullness of themselves. Yet they are unwilling to make the hard climb against self that you just experienced. You now know the limiting factor of self, and you have crossed this barrier that Satan employs so insidiously among my people."

Ask group members what they understood from this story. Get their ideas. Mention that as you climb higher, instead of letting fear and "self" grab greater control, you must depend on Christ. Then you will begin to see his reflection staring back at you from the Mirrored Mountains. You must depend on him more and more to get you to the top. When you get really high, terror can kick in, and this is when you most need to let Jesus take over. Then you will see more and more of his reflection in the glass. The main point is that your "me" retreats to the back seat of your life so that Jesus is preeminent and clearly visible in who you are.

Moses and Meekness

Ask group members who was the meekest man who ever lived. The answer is Moses. (See Numbers 12:3.) Many would not think of Moses as being meek, since he led the multitude of Israelites across the desert for forty years to the Promised Land.

But in reality, Moses, from the moment of his encounter with God in the burning bush, put himself away and let God do all the leading. He illustrates how meekness makes a life so effective for the Lord. This selfless servant most likely experienced more face-to-face conversations with God than any other biblical character besides Jesus. Their dialogues were sincere, honest, and heart to heart. The Bible says they conversed "as a man speaks to a friend" (Exodus 33:11). This relationship was possible because of Moses' absolute meekness before his Lord and because of his daily determination to fulfill God's instructions, whatever they might be. Moses' meekness enabled the young nation of Israel to reach the Promised Land and then, through God's leadership in Joshua, to claim the Promised Land, the inheritance bequeathed to Abraham centuries before. Meekness will always produce an inheritance. What inheritance will our meekness win for others?

Play the music video "*It Must Be You*" by Bart Millard about Moses from *The Story*. The message of this song is the mind-set of meekness. (Music video begins on next slide)

Now comment that, like Moses, we must daily seek God to direct and oversee our duties and guide every planned and spontaneous interaction. Our primary desire is that all our decisions be in accordance with his perfect will and with his perfect purpose for us.

Jesus passionately told his disciples, "My food is to do the will of him who sent me, and to accomplish his work" (John 4:34). We are not to seek our own glory. Jesus said, "He who speaks from himself seeks his own glory" (John 7:18 NASB). Everything that Jesus did on this earth was done to bring glory to his Father. The attitude of his prayers was, "Father, I am wholly yours today as always. Use me as you see fit." That should be our daily attitude also. What passion it will give us to live each day! This reemphasizes the importance of our daily encounter with Our Lord.

Jesus Is the Light—Let Him Shine through You!

Jesus declared, "I am the light of the world; he who follows me shall not walk in darkness, but have the light of life" (John 8:12). For the light of Christ to illuminate our path and shine through us to others, we must diminish, and his light must increase. Our Messiah did not seek the approval of man, and nor should we. Meekness allows his light to come to full brilliance in us.(*the image of Christ becomes larger in this slide*)

What was one of Jesus' greatest demonstrations of meekness? The night before his death when he humbly washed his disciples' feet. As Jesus gently washed the dirt and grime from their feet, the disciples' prideful natures were also dislodged, except in the case of Judas. As they led the early church, their thoughts must often have returned to that night, to the tender touch of their Master, to his example of meekness, and to the privilege they enjoyed in relating personally to the living Savior. These experiences drove them to take each step forward in meekness exactly as Jesus directed to establish his church in this world.

The essence of meekness is the crucifixion of our prideful nature. Our world is to revolve around Christ, not us. Any me-first attitude must become "me after God" as we permit him to come fully to life within us. Such an orientation will lead us in only one direction, the right one—toward God's will for our lives. We will be steadily centered on him and how we are to fulfill his purposes as we revel in his blessings and anticipate the day he will say to us, "Well done, my good, faithful [and meek] servant. Enter into the kingdom of your Lord" (Matthew 25:21). We must follow in Christ's footsteps and move steadily forward to accomplish God's mission for our lives. Our lives become full of "less of me living" and more of God in us!

The Beatitude Moment for the Meek

Have a foot washing time, and let each group member wash at least one other member's feet while you play the song *So Far to Find You* by Casting Crowns. (Audio is on next slide) Then ask them to recount their feelings as they washed someone else's feet and share how they felt when their feet were being washed. How did their "me" feel? Did their meekness begin to increase? Imagine if Jesus was washing your feet, how would this have made you feel?"

Blessed are the meek!

Where meekness will lead you!

Be not consumed with self, and be filled daily with the gentle spirit, strength, and direction of Jesus Christ in your dealings and confrontations, and you will be conquerors of this world and heirs in the Kingdom of God.

God has a plan for each one of us. And his plan is our inheritance!

Blessed are the meek, those possessors of gentle strength who are dedicated, directed, and determined to reflect Christ here on earth. Their reward, both here and afterward, will be grander and richer than this world could ever know, understand, or appreciate, because they are living in heaven while on earth and experiencing God's original desire for intimate fellowship with his most treasured creation, us. Truly our vision of God's kingdom is becoming grander and our understanding deeper, but there is a ridge leading us upward even farther!

Thoughts for Meditation

- How have I walked humbly with my God today?
- Where does God want to lead me today?

- What land will my meekness attain for myself and for others?

Show this slide and ask: Does this statement really represent true meekness? Or the second picture of the lamb which appears?

Focus on God ….

Play the Beatitudes song *"Less of Me" sung by Bucky Heard.*

Closing Prayer from Galatians 2: 20 (NIV)

(Gather in a circle with all holding hands)

"I have been crucified with Christ and I no longer live, but Christ lives in me. The life I now live in the body, I live by faith in the Son of God, who loved me and gave himself for me." Amen.

Final comment: Can we attain total meekness on our own?

BEing the Beatitudes

Memorize this Beatitude and repeat it daily with the other two already studied. Reflect daily upon the Scripture verses listed at the end of this chapter. Relive the foot washing experience and consider how it affected you as a washer and as a wash-ee.

Blessed are those who hunger and thirst after righteousness, for they shall be filled (Matthew 5:6)

Read the Beatitude on the first slide,

Three Major Spiritual Distractions Are Now behind Us!

Ask group members what three spiritual distractions have the first three Beatitudes enabled us to conquer and vanquish. Each one can easily prevent us from experiencing a full relationship with our Lord.

These major distractions are:

- Our spiritual pride which keeps us from comprehending God's grandeur and greatness;
- Our tendency to dwell on and attempt to deal with our burdens and the emotions they produce within us instead of releasing them to our Lord;
- Our emphasis on our "me" in making decisions and living our lives.
- So where do we go from here? What should consume our being and doing? With these three major spiritual distractions cast aside, we now have only one major focus in our lives—
- Our desire to know God fully! And to be totally filled with him! Our Lord Jesus Christ, God our Father, and the Holy Spirit all desire to make themselves more fully known to us. The fourth Beatitude is all about allowing God to fill us with himself, enabling us to gain a greater

understanding of him, of what he has done for us, and of why he paid the painful price of sacrificing his only Son.

- Lord, fill us with YOU. Help us to understand more deeply your perfect love, mercy, and grace.

Righteousness Is God's Word

We now hunger and thirst after righteousness; it is our overwhelming motivation. But what exactly is righteousness? It is a difficult word to define in English. One definition is "living right before God." In Spanish, the word is simply translated as "justice," which makes it easier to understand. In this Beatitude we come to understand God's justice, which leads us to comprehend the depth of what he has done for us.

This Beatitude alerts us to God's exacting standard of holiness and justice. We see that the holy perfection of his justice requires that a penalty be paid for our sins against him. That punishment should require our death. Justice is getting what we deserve.

But God's Word also reveals his boundless mercy for us. He will not give us what we deserve as sinners and as offenders against his perfect law. Mercy is <u>not</u> receiving the punishment we deserve.

God decided to go far beyond his mercy and forgiveness and give us free grace. Grace is getting what we do not deserve! He has given us what we could never earn for ourselves, and has reconciled us with him and his perfect law. He has made all this possible because of his great love for us! And Jesus is the face of God's amazing grace!

We are destitute beggars receiving God's greatest gift! In Bangladesh, beggars on the street shout "buckshish", meaning "free gift"-- a perfect description of God's gift of grace to us.

So, how can we allow these great truths unfold before us and learn more about God even more profoundly? Through the great Word of God. This spiritual knowledge is stored up in an endless reservoir ready to be poured out to us! The Spirit of God opens up our hearts and our minds to unfathomable secrets through his Word.

The Written Word

Why does God provide the Bible for us? The Bible is God's written Word given by him to us through forty strikingly diverse authors over a span of 1,500 years with a singular, mighty, and magnificent purpose. Through his Word God declares his mission to redeem mankind, the formation of his special people as the nation of Israel, and then—with the coming of Christ—his church and children today.

King David paints a salivating picture of how we are to approach the Word. "How sweet are your words to my taste, sweeter than honey to my mouth" (Psalm 119:103 (NIV).

The prophet Jeremiah echoes the same great appetite for Scriptural nourishment, "Your words were found and I ate them. Thy words became for me a joy and the delight of my heart" (Jeremiah 15:16). We must deeply digest the Word of God to find spiritual and emotional nourishment.

("His Word" slide) Have a bowl of honey with crackers beside it so that group members can dip them into the honey.) Ask for their reaction to this great taste. Was the honey unexpectedly sweet? That is how discovering God's Word is!

God provided the Bible for our deepest and sweetest investigation. As we dwell on his Word, we come to fathom the depth and the perfection of his holy righteousness and of the magnificent treasures freely given us by Jesus Christ. What does it mean to digest the Word of God? What is the difference between learning the Word and experiencing the Word?

On the eve of his betrayal, Jesus told his disciples, "He who has my commandments and keeps them, he it is who loves me; and he who loves me shall be loved by my Father, and I will love him, and will disclose myself to him" (John 14:21). You can't know God and Jesus intimately without knowing his Word. The submission of our hearts to God's commandments is our primary expression of love for him. And a humble and meek heart attained in the previous Beatitude is the most responsive to the transforming power of the Word. God's written Word is one primary way we can know him better, but there is another Word! Diving into God's word is one way we prove our love for him, and come to know his kingdom more deeply.

His Word Living in Us!

John's inspired gospel account of Jesus starts this way: "In the beginning was the Word, and the Word was with God, and the Word was God." (John 1:1)

John 1:14 says, "Jesus was the Word who was made flesh and lived among us, and we beheld his glory, glory of the firstborn of the Father." Jesus personified all Scripture and the fulfilled the message of God from all ages. In John 6:63, he revealed what life is all about. "The words I have spoken to you are spirit and are life."

After feeding the multitude, Jesus proclaimed in John 6:35, "I am the bread of life. How do we partake of the "Bread of Life"? And remember that "the multitude was filled" and there were baskets left over!

Whoever comes to me will never go hungry, and

Whoever believes in me will never be thirsty." So as we saturate ourselves in God's written Word, the very Word himself, Jesus Christ, reveals it even further to us! The more we discover about righteousness the more our souls will become enlightened to a greater realization of all that Christ has accomplished for us.

We find giant treasure troves of righteousness in God's written Word and in the living Christ. From the written Word, we will absorb great truths as we are led by the Holy Spirit, who reveals them to our intellectual reasoning and our spiritual sensitivity. Yet righteousness is also attained in our daily relationship with Jesus Christ, who reveals great spiritual realities to us in our everyday experiences. The Word of God seeks to embrace us and fill us with its truth and spiritual strength.

We must hunger and thirst after both Words. Just imagine what you can absorb from both of them! Both Words becomes our world from this point forward in our quest through the remaining Beatitudes. Blessed are those who hunger and thirst to know God's justice—those who possess an insatiable appetite for God, not just as he is revealed in the Scriptures, but also as he can be experienced in a deeply personal way each day.

Maintain a Stay-Hungry Diet

Have someone read this passage from Matthew Henry's *Commentary on the Whole Bible (Complete)*.

> We must truly and really desire spiritual blessings, as one who is hungry and thirsty desires meat and drink, who cannot be satisfied with anything else, and will be only satisfied with them, though other things might be needed. Our desires of spiritual blessings must be earnest and fervent, "Give me these, or else I die! Everything else is unsatisfying. Give me these, and I have enough, though I have nothing else."

Hunger and thirst are appetites that return frequently, and call for fresh satisfactions; so these holy desires rest not in any thing attained, but carry us toward renewed pardons, and daily fresh supplies of grace. The quickened soul calls for constant meals of righteousness, grace to do the work of every day in its day, as duly as the living body daily calls for food.

Discover God in his Word!

We Are Constantly Fulfilled

Jesus promises that this passionate hunger and thirst for goodness and for holiness will be filled. We will not be left disappointed, distraught, or deprived. The result of hungering and thirsting for righteousness is not just being filled, but experiencing an overflowing fattening from God's holiness and goodness.

The Mystery of Christ. In the Bible, Jesus declared that true believers must eat his flesh and drink his blood, signifying the sacrificial price he had to pay for our sin. The atoning power of his crucifixion and resurrection are wrapped up in his flesh and blood. He desires that we comprehend this great mystery, which will become the principal driving force in our spiritual pilgrimage. Our understanding of Christ's sacrifice is inextricably linked to the depth of our passion, purpose, and path of life here on earth.

We are as starving baby birds in a nest, straining upward with hearts stretched wide open, hungry for heavenly knowledge. Behold, the Word of God comes and fills us, more satisfyingly than we ever dreamed possible. We feast upon his Word with an earnest desire and an effort to digest each morsel and passage. "He loves those who pursue righteousness" (Proverbs 15:9).

Study and Apply Every Scripture

As we pour over God's Word, we must ask ourselves, why did God write this? How does it apply to our lives right now? What is God's intention with each verse and passage? His Spirit will transport us to the greatest dimensions of understanding and to discover ourselves even more deeply. God uses his Word to reveal us to ourselves.

As Hebrews 4:12 says, "For the Word of God is living and active and sharper than any two-edged sword, and piercing as far as the division of soul and spirit, of both joints and marrow, and able to judge the thoughts and intentions of the heart."

The Word not only enables us to know God and ourselves better.…. but gives us increased strength against the evil one.

God's plan, his inheritance for us that is promised in the previous Beatitude, can be clearly discovered in his Word!

The Rich Ridge of Righteousness Becomes the Beatitude Moment for Those Who Hunger and Thirst after Righteousness

After the group looks at this picture, have the members close their eyes and imagine themselves in the middle of it as you read the following paragraph.

In the Land of the Beatitudes, after having submitted ourselves to the peaks of the Mirrored Mountains, we encounter a ridge leading to even higher ground. We proceed upward along the Rich Ridge of Righteousness where a smorgasbord of spiritual fruits lines our path. Upon closer examination, we discover that many of these delicacies are familiar verses, but that we have never tasted or experienced them to their true fullness and meaning. Towering trees abound all around us, heavily laden and inviting our indulgence. A crystal-clear stream offers eternal refreshment.

Distribute artificial flowers and have group members write a favorite memorized verse on a notecard and attach it to a flower with a string of yarn. Then lay the flowers out on the floor and have the members pick up each one and "discover" these verses on the Rich Ridge of Righteousness.

"Enjoy Your Verses" slide. Ask them: Which favorite verses did they already know? Which ones were new? Have them quote some. The goal is to help them understand that they probably don't know many by heart and need to cultivate a desire to do so.

Closing comment for this activity: "Do we simply taste of these spiritual fruits, or should we indulge ourselves and be filled?

Experience the Word!

On the Rich Ridge of Righteousness, we must maintain a stay-hungry diet for God's Word, even as we are filled to overflowing each day with his powerful truth and Spirit. This Beatitude is for all who hunger and thirst after God's righteousness. In his Word, we find in excess what we seek for nourishment and renewal. We discover more and more of his unchanging character as the Holy Spirit empowers us to absorb it. This is the joy of fulfillment—to feel the God of the universe and his Son speaking to the very center of our being in a powerfully personal way.

Memorizing Scripture is the best way to totally consume it and allow it to penetrate your heart, soul, and being, and be used by the Holy Spirit in times of weakness and need.

Play "*The Lamp*" by Charlie Hall, and have group members read the words while they listen. (Audio begins on this slide, as song verses proceed, continue forward with each slide.)

> The flowers will fade in their beauty, but your word travels faithful and true.
> My hands on the pulse I am listening, and the words come to life and they bloom.
> Oh, your word is a lamp to my path. Oh, your word is a lamp to my path.
>
> Let the power of your word dwell here richly, changing the way that I see.
> Fill me with otherly wisdom. Plant me deep like a tree by the stream.
> Oh, your word is a lamp to my path. Oh, your word is a lamp to my path.

Show the slide of the man amazed at the Word during the musical
interlude between the 2ⁿᵈ and 3ʳᵈ verses of "Lamp".
I don't put my hope in my wishes. I hang on your promises true.
Your word's like a sword searching all of my heart, dividing the lies from
the truth.
Oh, your word is a lamp to my path. Oh, your word is a lamp to my path.

Let the power of Your Word dwell here richly, changing the ways that
I see.
Fill me with otherly wisdom, plant me deep like a tree by the stream.
Your word is a lamp to my path. Your word is a lamp to my path.

Ask what is meant by "otherly wisdom" in the second verse. (It is wisdom directly from God obtained from his Word.) Quote this verse: "Seek ye first the kingdom of God and his righteousness and all these things will be added to you" *(Matthew 6:33).*

A Desperate Seeker of Righteousness

Who was one of the greatest seekers of righteousness in the Old Testament? What do you think of when you think of Job?

Play the music video *"Broken Praise"* from *The Story*, (Begin video on next slide) Share the following about Job's tragic experience before showing the video.

Job's highest priority was to seek God's righteousness. This was the empowering passion in Job's life. He would settle for nothing else. Even though all his children and earthly possessions had been taken, Job's cry was not for vindication and restoration. No, his obsession was a desperate hunger and thirst for God's righteousness, and to know Him ever more intimately. And God did reveal Himself mightily to his seeking servant through commanding and potent portraits of his power, authority, and justice. To all who intensely crave to know God, a wondrous reward of great saturation waits, because his greatest desire is to fill his children with Himself. (Beatitudes book pages 52-53)

Share this paragraph after showing the video:

Job was distraught and pleaded to know, "Why am I suffering so?" for 42 chapters. In the end God came to him personally and Job said to himself, "I despise myself, and repent in dust and ashes. Job realized how small he was in the presence of Almighty God. He grasped that the "created" cannot question the "Creator". We must trust our Creator. What changed Job's mind was his knowledge of and experience with God. Exactly was we have pilgrimaged in the first four Beatitudes. God did not answer Job's questions. There was no need to because God WAS Job's answer. That is why it is so important to come to know God as intimately as possible, because he is always our answer for everything.

Share this verse. "In the way of righteousness there is life; along that path is immortality" (Proverbs 12:28).

Be constant in your desire to understand the Word. Blessed are those who daily delve into it with a desperate desire to know God more deeply. They will!

Thoughts for Meditation

- What attribute of God's righteousness has he revealed to you today?
- How has God's Word changed your life today?

Lord Your Word is now in me!
Your Word in my world!
Show Focus on God…..
Play the Beatitude song, ***"Close to You" sung by Beyond the Ashes***

Final comment: How does our hunger and thirst for righteousness become a progressive need in a believer's life?

BEing the Beatitudes

Practice saying by memory the first four Beatitudes. Reflect daily upon the Scripture verses at the end of this chapter, and commit to memorizing one verse a week.

BETWEEN THE BEATITUDES: REFLECTING ON THE FIRST FOUR BEATITUDES

Ask group members these four strategic questions about how the first four Beatitudes have affected their lives and their relationships with God.

1) **The poor in spirit.** Does recognizing your spiritual poverty now make you feel richer in your relationship with God?

2) **Those who mourn.** Are you allowing Christ to carry all your burdens?

3) **The meek.** Have you put your "mighty me" in the back seat and now let Jesus drive your life?

4) **Those who hunger and thirst after righteousness.** Is knowing God now the priority of your life? Are you daily "in the Word" (Scripture) and "with the Word" (Jesus Christ)?

The "who" within yourself should have experienced a significant transformation by now. You should feel an even stronger relationship with God and have a deeper understanding of the first greatest commandment—to love the Lord with all your heart, all your soul, and all your mind. These four integral elements of who you are should have been dramatically impacted by the first four Beatitudes!

Four significant experiences still await us, but the previous four Beatitudes have prepared us for what lies ahead. We still have much to discover within ourselves and much to confess to God as we keep increasing in this spiritual sojourn. But even if we were to stop here, our relationship with God would never be the same, not just in comparison with yesterday, but also with tomorrow, because his holy and sacred fellowship will continue to transform every dimension of our lives.

Play "Constant" by Charlie Hall, and ask the group members to sing along. (Audio begins on this slide and continues with each verse slide)

Just like the sunshine, you have been our light, leading us into beautiful places.

We've walked through fire, but you've made us brighter, leading us into beautiful places.

Faithful Jesus, healing Savior, compass, center, Bread of Life.

Faithful Jesus, cherished treasure, Our portion, wisdom, God's great Light.

God, you are here with us, constantly here with us. You are our everything, faithful and true.

Just like the starlight, you shine in the black night, leading us into beautiful places.

Just like the atmosphere, you've come to surround us here, leading us into beautiful places.

Faithful Jesus, healing Savior, compass, center, Bread of Life.

Faithful Jesus, cherished treasure, Our portion, wisdom, God's great Light

A new dawning is here (with the first four Beatitudes) but a new day still awaits us (with the next four Beatitudes)!

Blessed are the merciful, for they shall receive mercy (Matthew 5:7)

Read this Beatitude together with the group and then comment: We really cannot be merciful until we have actually experienced God's mercy and it comes to reside within us. We must remember the radical change in our life that day "when mercy came". This Beatitude is about experiencing God's Mercy and letting His Mercy take over us.

A parable of Jesus. Play the video of "*Come Back Home*" by Kutless. (Music video begins on next slide.)

Ask the group if they recognize what Bible story this song is about—The Prodigal Son.

Ask group members what insights into God's mercy this parable offers. The key point is when the son "came to his senses" and realized that his only hope was to return home. Emphasize that no matter how far we've strayed from God, His mercy always forgives us <u>if</u> we have a truly repentant heart that desperately desires him.

Peter's Beatitude Moment

First summarize some of the major events representing Peter's impulsive personality as Jesus' disciple with the following slides:

In the storm, when he saw Jesus walking on water, Peter jumped out of the boat and he himself walked on water as long as he gazed as Jesus. Then the fear of the storm struck him and he sank into the turbulent waves. But Jesus came over quickly to rescue him.

In Caesarea of Philippi when Jesus asked his disciples, "Who do you say that I am?" Peter immediately responded, "You are the Messiah, the Son of God." But later in that same conversation as Jesus foretold his imminent death in Jerusalem, Peter objected to his master that nothing like this could happen to the Messiah. Jesus promptly responded to Peter, "Get behind me Satan."

The night of his betrayal when Jesus washed his disciples' feet, Peter refused to allow Jesus to wash his feet. Jesus responded, then you will have nothing to do with me. Peter immediately changed his mind and said, "Not just my feet, wash all of me."

Shortly afterward that same evening when Jesus advised Peter that Satan would sift him like wheat and that he would deny his Master three times. Peter picked up a sword and declared, "I will die for you, and defend you to my death."

Later in Gethsemane, Peter cut off a Roman soldier's ear, which Jesus ordered Peter to drop his sword and gently replaced the detached ear back on the soldier's head.

Peter shrank into the shadows and followed the entourage to the courtyard where Jesus would be tried by the Hebrew religious authorities.

There, while waiting, he was accused by three different people of being a disciple of Jesus, and he vehemently denied each accusation. At his third denial, the rooster crowed, and Jesus, in the midst of his torture and suffering, turned and looked Peter in the eye.

Peter melted in the gaze of his master and rushed out the courtyard overcome with guilt and shame and emotional pain. He roamed the streets for three days wallowing in grief and remorse over his denial of Jesus. On the third day He ran behind Mary and Martha to the grave, and saw the empty tomb.

Later that same day Jesus appeared to Peter alone, and flooded him with his mercy of forgiveness over him. Peter was amazed and dramatically changed by Jesus' mercy poured over him.

Whether we stray, like the Prodigal Son or betray, like Peter, God's mercy will find us. Just as the father expectantly awaits the return of his prodigal son, Jesus awaits with mercy the arrival or the return of every saint. God's mercy is proof of his unconditional love. He reaches out to us, no matter what. We may not be as desperate or as bold in our betrayal or denial as Peter was, but we will all commit grave sin, because all sin is grave to God, and sin is our graveyard. We all urgently require his mighty resurrection mercy to move us forward in life and in this quest.

Mercy Means New Life

Ask the students to define *mercy*. List some of their ideas. (Unconditional love, total pardon, and forgiveness, hopefully, will be mentioned.) Discuss the confusion between the words "pity" and "mercy". Pity is feeling sorrow for someone. Mercy is true forgiveness for what they have done. With God, mercy allows us to start anew. Our closeness with the Written and Living Word from the previous Beatitude enables us to grasp at even greater depths God's intense mercy, completed through Jesus' life and death on earth in which he voluntarily came to die in our place and give us new life.

His mercy gifts new life for each one of us.

Jesus declared in John 11:25-26, "I am the resurrection and the life; he who believes in me shall live, even if he dies, "and everyone who lives and believes in me shall never die."

Do you believe this?"

Jesus left his power and position in heaven for you and me. Perhaps he had glimpses of those strolls through eternity during his human pilgrimage on earth, confirming his desire to carry out the sacrifice that would assure you and me that same heavenly home. Jesus descended from his pure celestial homeland to the filthy sewer of this sinful world to be subjected to an excruciating death by the very ones he came to save. Yet Jesus was willing to undergo this terrible torment for me and for you. This is his merciful gift of love to us—to resurrect us to life in his spiritual realm. His sole desire is to give new life, a new beginning to a world without end, and an intimate closeness to the God of all creation! Is not that astounding? He offers this extreme love to the very creation that betrayed and turned its back on him. How many gods would die for their rebellious creation? Only One, whose love is the essence of mercy!

The Dark Caverns of Mercy

We have all been imprisoned in the Dark Caverns of Mercy, before we experienced God's mercy. Trapped in darkness and ignorant of our need for God. He enabled his great mercy to extend specifically to souls lost and frantically groping in the deep and dark caverns of life—those who are in desperate need of God's great reaching down. Perhaps they have tried to live good lives, but as we know, goodness does not win eternal life.

Thankfully, these caverns have an escape route—the great forgiving mercy of Jesus, who reaches down to rescue us. Just as he did with Peter, Jesus longs to have a personal experience with every lost soul and separated saint to bring them back home and grant them a new and resurrected life. Many people wander in unbelief and ignorance in the darkness, unaware that they're even lost, but fully conscious that something is missing in their lives.

Do you remember specifically God's great reaching down for you? Him knocking on the door of your heart? Your personal encounter with Christ? If it was not personal a truly personal experience, it was not real, but it can be right now!

Recapture and recreate the spiritual process of that moment.

- The intensely convicting power of the Holy Spirit knocking on your heart.
- Your deep recognition of and sincere repentance for your sin.
- True understanding that only Jesus can save you from your sin.
- Inviting Jesus to come into your life and heart and reside forever.

The Beatitude Moment for the Merciful

Play the song "Mercy" by Casting Crowns. (Audio on this slide) Ask group members to relive their own salvation moment as they listen to this song. Remember it as if was yesterday. You, as the group leader, could share your own salvation moment with the group to help set the tone for this important time of reflection.

This would also be a perfect moment to ask if someone present has not had this salvation experience, the most important decision in life. If someone says that he has not yet met Christ personally, follow the Spirit's leadership and bring him to our Lord right there or invite him to talk with you privately after the lesson is over.

Where Does Mercy Lead Us?

The Greek word for *mercy* in this Beatitude means "to feel sympathy with the misery of another, to have compassion abiding in one's heart, to show kindness by benevolence, to help the afflicted, and to bring help to the wretched." Emphasize that mercy is feeling and responding.

These responses convey an unwavering willingness by someone rich in resources to selflessly reach out and rescue a person with no other recourse. God did this for us, even though we were blindly unaware of our misery in sin, our wretched lack of holiness, and our desperate need for salvation. Remember our poverty from the first Beatitude—we can't find salvation on our own! He sent Jesus to pay our price, seek us out, and save us once and for all. This Beatitude actually involves two steps of mercy. First is the wondrous heavenly mercy that rescues those in need, just as Jesus Christ came to deliver us from our sinful and lost condition. Second is the mercy that compels us, as children of God, to extend that same mercy to others. We became mercy-full when Jesus Christ entered our hearts and lives.

Consider how Peter's mercy encounter with Christ affected countless lives in his future ministry. As he proclaimed to the crippled man in Acts 3:6, "Silver and gold I do not have, but what I have I give to you. In the name of Jesus Christ of Nazareth, get up and walk." Mercy also invigorated his spiritual power to heal Aneas and raise Dorcas from the dead. God's vision to Peter on the roof enlarged his spiritual tent, showing him that the mercy of the gospel was meant for the Gentiles, as well as the Jews, a concept far beyond his previous mentality. And he immediately sought out Cornelius, the Roman centurion. Peter's mercy magnified his ministry and touched many lives. It was not a treasure stored up inside him, but flowed through him to countless others. So should be our lives for Christ. God's mercy extends our ministry to others.

Mercy is the primary motivating element of God's great grace to us, and after we become his children, we are authentically infused with his unconditional love, and we are propelled to manifest it to others. We cannot resist. As living instruments of his mercy on earth, we are obliged to allow that mercy to spill out to all those around us. We are not just mercy-filled, but mercy-flooded! We cannot contain it! We must possess a mercy mentality that is possible only when Jesus lives in us!

Extend Mercy to All in Your Path

As we encounter people each day, we must ask, how can I allow Jesus to use me to display God's great mercy gift to them? We must explain to them that the cross of Christ is the symbol of God's great love for them. Often we may be their only reference point for that love. We must be the true north to them, take their hands, and lead them to the Savior we know so well so that they, too, can experience God's great mercy gift! We have been given the great privilege to direct them from darkness into his marvelous light, though each individual has the opportunity to reject or to accept this glorious gift. Mercy is now our way of life—just like Jesus lived on earth!

Blessed are the mercy-full, who have experienced God's great reaching down.

His mercy in us can make grand differences in lives every day.

Show the music video "*When Loves Sees You*" by Mac Powell from *The Story*.(Music video is on the next slide Ask the group to discuss how this video depicts Jesus' mercy wherever he went, whatever he experienced, however he was treated.

Read Micah 6:8, which says, "He has told you, O man, what is good; and what does the Lord require of you but to do justice, **love mercy**, and walk humbly with your God?"

Play "Micah 6:8" by Charlie Hall, and challenge group members to memorize this key Scripture passage, which tells us how God wants us to live.

Become immersed in his mercy and be filled with the great goodness of God toward all those he places in your path.

Closing Prayer of Mercy from 1 Timothy 1:15-17

(Form a circle and hold hands as someone leads this prayer.)

Here is a trustworthy saying that deserves full acceptance: Christ Jesus came into the world to save sinners—of whom I am the worst. But for that very reason I was shown mercy so that in me, the worst of sinners, Christ Jesus might display his immense patience as an example for those who would believe in him and receive eternal life. Now to the king eternal, immortal, invisible, the only God, be honor and glory forever and ever. Amen.

Thoughts for Meditation

- Where do you see and feel God's mercy most in your life today?
- How will you display his mercy to others today?

Show slide with summary of this Beatitude.
Play the Beatitudes song, ***"When Mercy Came" sung by Annette Herndon.***

Final comment: Describe the blessings of the merciful.

BEing the Beatitudes

Memorize this Beatitude, and add it to the others already committed to memory. Reflect daily upon the verses listed for the merciful, and let God lead you to memorize those verses that speak most powerfully to your heart.

Blessed are the pure in heart, for they shall see God (Matthew 5:8)

Have the group read this Beatitude together and then tell them, our spiritual quest has brought us to this pivotal and most challenging Beatitude of all.

We recognize our spiritual poverty, have crucified our spiritual pride, and magnified the majesty of God.

We have released our burdens to Jesus, come to the Well, and now completely depend on him.

We have submitted ourselves to more of Him and less of me living. Self is now in the back seat of our lives.

We maintain a "stay-hungry feast" for God's Word—his Written Word and Christ living in us.

We have received God's great mercy gift of grace due to the sacrificial death of his Son for us. Our comprehension of his love has exponentially expanded, and now that same mercy flows through us to the world!

What can possibly be left for us to experience? There is still more to come—especially from this Beatitude!

Comment that purity is pureness with no defilement. We should strive to achieve total purity before God. Not perfection, which we can never attain, but an assuredness that we are holding nothing back before Our Lord!

How Pure Is Our Heart before God?

We must ask ourselves, "How pure is our heart before God? Remember that our heart is the essence of who we are in every dimension of our life.

Proverbs 4:23 states, "Above all else, guard your heart, for everything you do flows from it." Our heart is the most essential aspect of who we are.

As you share the following, emphasize the underlined words and phrases:

At the end of our physical life, after the last pulse and push of blood through our body, we will stand before God in his great throne room to reveal the true nature of our being. God will closely examine <u>our spiritual heart</u>, which is the reality of <u>who we are</u>—not merely on the surface to others, but down to the <u>very core of our being</u>.

Proverbs 17: 3 explains, "The refining pot is for silver and the furnace for gold, but the Lord tests hearts." What impurities in our life will surface? God continually searches for pure, undefiled hearts that are right toward him.

Our heart houses <u>our values</u>. It is the <u>decision center of right and wrong</u> for us. It determines our <u>behavior</u> and how we relate to others. It <u>directs our thought life</u> and what we dwell on. It <u>empowers our personality</u> and who we are toward others. Our heart dictates the decisions we make in life, both good and bad.

Before our Creator, we will stand "heart naked" and stripped bare to reveal the real nature of our being. A pure heart, according to God's standards, will be found worthy. As Proverbs 16:2 declares, "All a man's ways seem innocent to him, but motives are weighed by the Lord." Before God and before the Beatitudes this is our most likely way to react—thinking that our ways are innocent, but can we truly identify every motive of ours? God certainly can. Do we really possess a pure heart before God?

The Purging Valley of the Pure in Heart

In this difficult and possibly painful valley we must each ask ourselves, "Is my heart completely pure before God?"

Pure as used in this Beatitude conveys powerful ideas in the original Greek *kathros*: a genuine, innocent, and blameless heart free from corrupt desire, sin, and guilt, purified by fire, free of defilements of the flesh and of the world; a clear and transparent heart. This is quite a list to live up to!

A pure heart is solely and wholly committed to one goal: to please only God in all one <u>thinks, does, and says</u>. That's an extremely high standard for humans in this sin-filled world! We must honestly evaluate our hearts by the *kathros* standard!

Challenge ahead!

Pose the following questions to the group members.

Have you ever experienced a surgical procedure? Do you remember that massive light beaming down upon you? This Beatitude is spiritual open heart surgery.

God's pure and intense light will reveal any impurities, secret or hidden sin lying encrusted there. Some sins are too difficult to shed alone—it is easier to pretend that they aren't there or just keep living with them. Some sins lie dormant and unconfessed, perhaps affecting your attitude toward someone else even today. Perhaps you are not even aware of a concealed sin, but God desires to reveal it to you today.

Today is the day to remove any and all sin to yield a pure heart before God.

Play "My Own Worst Enemy" by Casting Crowns, (music video on the next slide) and then discuss the song's message. Pride is our greatest spiritual enemy that Satan uses most effectively. But even though we put our "mighty me" in the back seat in the Beatitude of meekness, it continually strives to crawl back into the driver's seat of our lives.

The Beatitude Moment for the Pure in Heart

It's time to bare your heart before God. Dim the lights and provide space between participants so that they can have private and intimate time with God during these next few minutes.

Guide their time of prayer with these statements from the slide:

- Lord, please reveal the true condition of my heart to me. Are there any impurities before you, Lord? Please reveal them to me! Help make my heart pure before you!
- Is there any unconfessed sin in my life? Please give me the courage to confess it to you!
- Is there any bitterness, resentment, or anger toward others that I need to leave before you? Lord, give me your forgiving spirit toward that person!
- Is there a vice or an addiction that won't let me go? I call upon the power of your Holy Spirit to remove it from my life!
- Lord, if there is some hidden sin of which I am unaware, please reveal it to me! Help me see it through your eyes and confess it before you!
- Please reveal to me anything that is separating me from a full relationship with you!

Tell them that as they pray:

- You must sincerely confess to God whatever he reveals to you. Ask him to forgive you, to take control of this sin or vice, and to remove it from your heart and your life.
- This could (and should) be an intensely emotional experience for all who are serious about purifying their relationships with God. This is the moment when you enter true oneness with him. It isn't easy. You must turn anything impeding that relationship over to God—you cannot take care of it on your own! God will gladly take over it for you.

Play "At Your Feet" by Casting Crowns (audio on slide). Have an altar call and let group members come forward as they feel led to the altar or the cross and surrender their impurities to God. Lead the group in a prayer of thanksgiving to God for his great love in forgiving and cleansing us and making us one with him.

Once We Have Obtained a Pure Heart from God, How Can We Keep It Pure?

It is a mighty step to make our heart pure. Another major challenge is keeping it pure! The Scriptures give us very practical spiritual advice as to how we can stay pure before God once we have attained his heart. We certainly don't want to lose it!

In his book *What Every Christian Ought to Know,* Pastor Adrian Rodgers explains that our human nature is composed of three parts—body, soul, and spirit—and that Satan is the expert at knowing how to tempt each one. After all, he's been doing it since the dawn of man.

1 John 2:15-17 declares that sin will attack us in three major areas. "For everything in the world—the lust of the flesh, the lust of the eyes, and the pride of life—comes not from the Father, but from the world."

- The lust of the flesh attacks our physical body with our own sinful nature.
- The lust of the eyes attacks our soul, the center of our psychological, emotional, and intellectual self, with worldly enticements—power, money, and prestige.
- The pride of life is an attack on our spirit by Satan himself, exploiting our pride and self—sufficiency. He enticed Adam and Eve to their fall in exactly this way.

How do we combat these three major areas of temptation? The Bible has the answers. *Against the flesh we are **to flee**.* In 2 Timothy 2:22, Paul states, "Flee also youthful lusts," and in 1 Corinthians 6:18, "Flee sexual immorality." Our spiritual common sense directs us to remove ourselves from any tempting environment and to avoid bad ones in the first place. We must be spiritually sensitive to what we look at, listen to, and read, and in what we absorb ourselves.

Avoidance is the best precaution for fleshly temptations. We must not give our fleshly nature an opportunity to work its cravings on us.

*Against the world we must **exercise faith**.* As children of God, we know that we will never find real satisfaction in what this world offers and promotes. There is no point searching the world to find spiritual satisfaction. As 1 John 2:15 tells us, "If anyone loves the world, the love of the Father is not in him." Our spiritual transformation through Christ, and the new life that it produces, protect us from seeing the attractions of the world as meaningful. Our treasures are not found in this world. We must commit to preparing treasures in heaven. Rely on the Lord you so well know. <u>Exercise faith</u> in him!

*Against the temptations of the spirit we are **to fight***. We must depend entirely on Jesus. We cannot permit Satan to create a wedge between us and God by manipulating our false pride, bitterness, or persistent grudges toward others. Believers are vulnerable in this area because we can easily think we are okay when we are following all of religion's rules. Satan eases himself into our complacency and creates a sense of pride in us that can distance us from God, just as he did to David before he committed his great sin with Bathsheba.

We must <u>fight, deny Satan, and tell him to get behind us</u>.

The Bible gives us clear counsel as to how we must respond. James 4:7 tells us, "Resist the devil and he will flee," while James 4:8 assures us, "Draw near to God, and he will draw near to you!" The instant we realize what the Evil One is about, we must declare, as Jesus did in Matthew 16:22-24, "Get behind me, Satan! You are a stumbling block to me; you do not have in mind the concerns of God, but merely human concerns." We must get away from Satan and run to Jesus. He is our rescue.

To be fully prepared to combat these temptations, the Word of God and his righteousness must be ever present in our minds for the Spirit to employ in our thoughts, hearts, and wills. Our "stay-hungry feast" should assure that His Word is active in our hearts and minds.

"Sin befogs and beclouds the heart so that one cannot see God. Purity clears and clarifies the senses and gives vision to everything," as Archibald T. Robertson writes in *Robertson's Word Pictures of the New Testament*.

The Bible assures us that no temptation shall overwhelm us. As 1 Corinthians 10:13 promises, "No temptation has overtaken you except such as is common to man; but God is faithful, who will not allow you to be tempted beyond what you are able, but when you are tempted he will also provide a way out so that you can endure it."

Always look for the way out! God will guide you through all temptation. Now you know the Godly exit from the three temptations that will beset us in this world, so get away from them fast! Flee, Exercise Faith, and Fight Satan!

A Prayer for the Pure in Heart from Psalm 24:3-5

Who may ascend into the hill of the Lord? And who may stand in his holy place? He who has clean hands and a pure heart, who has not lifted up his soul to falsehoods, and has not sworn deceitfully. He shall receive a blessing from the Lord and righteousness from the Lord of his salvation. (Psalms 23:3)

Hold up your heart before God.

David's Beatitude moment. Emphasize that this psalm was written by King David, who experienced a powerful purifying process after his sin with Bathsheba. Discuss David's Beatitude moment described pages 86-92 of the Beatitudes book, before showing the music video about him (next slide). It was David's driving heartbreak and desire to reestablish his fellowship with his Lord that called out to God and opened the door to re-purify and intensify his relationship with him.

Show "Your Heart" by Chris Tomlin from *The Story*.

Transparent Relationships with All Those around Us Too!

A pure heart begins with finding and maintaining a transparent love relationship with God as Jesus described in the first and greatest commandment. But he followed that with the second-most important commandment of the law and the prophets: we must love our neighbor as ourselves. In these last two Beatitudes, not only has our relationship with God further intensified, but we have been equally challenged to apply these spiritual realities with our fellow man. A pure heart is essential in our relationships with others. All barriers with others must be decimated.

In Matthew 5:23-24, Jesus instructed that anyone desiring to place an offering at the altar and worship God first examine his own heart. Any offense harbored toward a neighbor must first be reconciled before presenting an offering to God. In Matthew 18:35, Jesus emphasizes that the restoration of our relationships with others must be genuine. "This [judgment] is how my heavenly Father will treat each of you unless you forgive your brother or sister from your heart."

This spiritual law decreed by Christ certainly applies to us today, especially to those committed to living out the Beatitude of the pure in heart. Self is totally sacrificed before God and must not interfere with our relationships. They must be clean, sure, and unsoiled.

If you know you have offended someone or even if you were the one offended, you are obligated to resolve that conflict and not wait for the other person to take the initiative. The Spirit of Christ prompts and directs you to take the actions required to maintain a pure heart before God and man. You cannot knowingly ignore any unresolved problem with others and expect your heart to be clean before the Lord or them!

Have the group members close their eyes and reflect on their relationships. Are there any that need reconciliation or restoration? Have they purposely or accidentally offended someone and need to ask that person's forgiveness? The purity of each relationship should be evaluated. If they identify problems, they should determine what action is necessary to make things right. They must pray that God directs their thoughts and actions to bring this reconciliation to pass.

Conclusion

A pure heart is genuine, loving and totally transparent before both God and man. They see him clearly and see the world as he sees it too. This is the abundant life for which Jesus died to make possible for us and is the Garden of Eden fellowship that God sent Jesus to re-create with man. This high and holy fellowship will generate purity in relationships with all those around us. Jesus living fully in us gives life that we never could have imagined. What better way can there be to accomplish our days on this earth than to see God more clearly and commune with him more fully in each moment? This godly communion enriches all of our other relationships.

Be pure in heart, confess your sin and truly come to know God face to face. Forgive others, embracing those who have wronged you, and also, all those who you have wronged.

The path now leads only upward in our relationship with the Lord. Some treacherous stretches loom ahead in our Beatitude quest, and they will challenge us to become even more the people he wants us to be. We must be inspired by how far God has brought us and be encouraged to continue on to where Jesus yearns to carry us still!

Play "Center" by Charlie Hall (audio on slide). Give members opportunities to share how the "pure in heart" experience has affected them and/or how the song "Center" reflects the attitude of this Beatitude.

Thoughts for Meditation

- Have you laid your heart bare before the Lord today?
- Are there obstacles in any human relationships that you need to address?

Lord, let my heart be a rainbow to everyone I meet to show your colors in my life! Fellowship fully with You Lord….

Play the Beatitude song, *"Make Me Pure" sung by David Staton.*

BEing the Beatitudes

Be transparent daily before God, confess and ask forgiveness, maintain a habitual life of total honesty before him. Memorize this Beatitude along with the previous ones. Reflect daily upon the verses for this week. Memorize any that God specifically lays on your heart. Seek continual restoration in all your earthly relationships.

Blessed are the peacemakers, for they are the children of God (Matthew 5:9)

On the introductory slide for this lesson after reading the Peacemaker Beatitude comment that this Beatitude is not just about "making peace," but bringing peace to earth through the Good News of Jesus Christ, as his children!

Play a portion of the song "Jesus, Friend of Sinners" by Casting Crowns (audio on slide with pictures of Jesus that appear automatically), and ask the group what they consider to be the key lyric in this song: "Break my heart for what breaks yours."

Reflect upon how we have arrived at the point where our heart reflects the very love and passion of Our Lord. Those who hunger and thirst after righteousness sake, are living in the Word and with the Word. The Holy Spirit reveals to us more each day the deep truths of the Bible and the Mystery of Christ. God's Word is now our world!

We have received God's mercy with now floods and flows through us.

We now possess a pure heart, and we see our world as he sees it. When you have a pure heart before God, you are truly his child and view the world with the same compassion as Our Lord.

The "pure in heart" become his peacemakers. We are pieces of his peace on this earth. You have restored all broken relationships and are now in the peacemaking business for our Lord! As his children we are never peacebreakers, always peacemakers!

Remember that we are now rainbows of his love, showing his colors everywhere we go. There was such a person used by God as a mighty rainbow in a pivotal part of his plan to reveal himself here on earth.

Joseph, a great instrument of peace

Share with the group the story of Joseph from the beginning of the Peacemaker chapter (pages 109-118) using the following slides and narratives to illustrate this story.

Joseph was greatly favored from his very beginning, first by his father, who gave him a beautiful multicolored coat, and also by God, who enabled him to interpret his own dreams and those of others. An early dream was that his brothers were represented a sheaves of barley bowing down to him in a field.

This special recognition by his father and revelation of the dream made his brothers insanely jealous—so jealous, in fact, that they plotted to kill him by abandoning him in a pit where they hoped wild animals would devour him. Then, after one brother's appeal, they changed their minds and opted to sell Joseph to slave traders in a caravan traveling to Egypt.

Then they returned home and showed their father Joseph's multicolored tunic spattered with blood they had placed on it, and telling him that their brother had been killed by a wild beast. This broke Jacob's heart and intensified his love for Benjamin, Joseph's only brother born of the same mother, Racheal.

In Egypt, Joseph's master, Potipher, who quickly discerned his good and sincere heart, made him the steward (manager) of his home. Although Potipher's wife attempted numerous times to seduce Joseph, he repeatedly refused her. She became so enraged that she finally accused him of attacking her. This angered Potipher and he had Joseph thrown in prison.

The jail keeper also perceived Joseph's good heart and responsible attitude, and eventually placed him in charge of all prisoners. Joseph made every effort to comfort them in the face of their horrifying circumstances and the fate that might await them. He also interpreted dreams for some of them. Pharaoh's baker and cupbearer were suspected of an assassination attempt and were sentenced to prison. Both had dreams that they shared with Joseph. He foretold the cupbearer's sudden release and, sadly, the baker's imminent and gruesome execution.

Sometime after the cupbearer's release, Pharaoh was besieged with troubling dreams that no one could interpret, not even his wisest palace sages. The cupbearer remembered Joseph from prison and told Pharaoh about him. He immediately ordered Joseph to be brought before him. Without hesitation and fully crediting God for his gift of interpretation, Joseph clarified the meaning of each of Pharaoh's dreams. He also offered wise strategies to prepare Egypt for the approaching seven-year famine.

Pharaoh was so impressed with Joseph's great faith, his supreme God, and his wise ideas that he appointed him as second in command over all of Egypt to lead preparations for the famine. From a slave to a prisoner to a great position of power, Joseph was God's instrument, as also foreshadowed Jesus' life on earth.

The famine extended well beyond Egypt, encompassing much of the known world. One day Joseph's brothers, having traveled all the way from Canaan, unexpectedly appeared before him in court, pleading for food to take back to their families. Joseph immediately recognized them, yet chose not to reveal himself. He granted them their request, but to assure their return and apply a degree of justice for their earlier lawless acts, he kept one brother prisoner and sent the rest home laden with food. The brothers swore to return and bring their youngest brother, Benjamin, Joseph's only blood brother, as he insisted. Unknown to them, Joseph also ordered that the money they brought to purchase the food be placed back in the brothers' bags to save his father these expenses. They discovered this upon arriving home and were greatly perplexed.

Unbeknownst to the brothers, as they bowed before Joseph in respect and reverence, pleading for help, they were fulfilling the dream of his childhood—the sheaves bowing down before his sheaf.

After an extended period, the brothers finally returned with Benjamin. They attempted to return to Joseph the money that had been placed in their bags; however, he refused to take it and credited it to God. Joseph was impressed with this sign of integrity by them.

He warmly greeted his brother, Benjamin, and asked about his father, who his brothers reported was still in good health and was anxiously awaiting their return. Joseph gave them a scrumptious feast in which they were seated in their birth order which greatly puzzled them.

On their departure from the city, Joseph decided to test them again. He ordered that his special silver cup be hidden in Benjamin's bag. Joseph's soldiers stopped the brothers on the outskirts of the city. They were brought back before him and accused as thieves. Judah, who was Joseph's oldest brother who had masterminded his enslavement, stepped forward to plead fervently for Benjamin's freedom. He volunteered to take Benjamin's place and become Joseph's prisoner for life. Tearfully, Judah expressed deep concern that if Benjamin did not return home his father would die from grief. Judah had sworn by his life to his father Benjamin's safe return.

Discerning that Judah's ruthless heart had been transformed to good, Joseph finally revealed himself to them as their long-lost brother. What an emotional reunion they experienced! Joseph assured them that what they had intended for evil, the Lord God had transformed into good. "You sold me, but God sent me!" Joseph's great and good heart could always sense the "big picture".

Joseph and Pharaoh then directed the brothers to bring Joseph's father and his entire household to settle in Egypt to be sheltered from the famine.

Joseph humbly allowed himself to be used as the pivotal instrument to make possible the upcoming formation of God's people in Goshen to fulfill his promise to Abraham. His forgiving heart and sensitive spirit coupled with caring and responsible actions made him an extremely effective peacemaker in every challenge he faced. Joseph served as a vital bridge in God's plan for his people, and a foreshadowing of the love and peacemaking mission of Christ on earth.

Joseph was used by God to put into place the formation of his people in to a nation. From Joseph and his brothers, the Hebrews, God's own people, were formed in Egypt as the house of Jacob enlarged during a four hundred-year span.

Challenge the members to consider how Joseph's peacemaking principles can apply to our own lives. After they have offered some answers, ask them, "Who is the primary peacemaker in the history of man? The obvious answer for any Christian is Jesus, because he reconciled all of mankind with God. All generations of mankind were separated from God due to Adam and Eve's deliberate sin in the Garden of Eden, but were given a way back to their Creator through the peacemaking power of Jesus Christ.

Conclude by saying that when the spirit of Jesus reigns in our lives and we are pure in heart, as we see in Joseph's life, we will become peacemakers on this earth through the power of Jesus in us.

Peacemaking Principles from Proverbs

Comment that Peacemaking certainly demands and demonstrates meekness.

Share these verses about peacemaking from the book of Proverbs. "A gentle answer turns away wrath," "a soothing tongue is a tree of life," and "pleasant words are pure" (Proverbs 15:1, 4:26 NASB).

Proverbs 16:32 NASB instructs, "He who is slow to anger is better than the mighty. And he who rules his spirit, than he who captures a city." Proverbs 16:32 NASB reveals the powerful preference for peacemaking:

"Better is a dish of vegetables where love is, than a fattened ox and hatred with it." Proverbs 15:17 NASB

The adage "An eye for an eye, and a tooth for a tooth" (Exodus 24:24) is considered biblical justification for vengeance, but in reality it was meant to keep injured parties from exceeding the wrong done to them.

Jesus, the incarnate Word of God, voiced God's perspective on revenge as part of the Sermon on the Mount. "But I tell you do not resist an evil person. If someone strikes you on the right cheek, turn to him the other also" (Matthew 5:39). We took care of this human response in the 3rd Beatitude (*meekness*). Jesus desires to attract mankind to him through supernatural expressions of love and concern by his children made possible by his Spirit working in us!

An emotional knee-jerk reaction, although natural and seemingly justifiable, is not the way of God. Often, even as believers, resisting our normal human reactions is difficult in a world where gossip, arguments, fighting, and criticism are a way of life and only perpetuate more of the same. Human nature tends to rebel at the imposition of godly grace in our interactions with others, but as God's children we are commanded to leave behind any mind-set of superiority and diminishing others' worth.

Philippians 2:3 instructs, "Do nothing out of selfish ambition or vain conceit. Rather, in humility value others above yourselves."

Jesus broke the paradigm of normal human reactions when he commanded in Matthew 5:43, "Love your neighbors, and pray for those who persecute you in order that you might be sons of your Father in heaven."

The Beatitudes challenge, compel, and enable us to live out the second-greatest commandment, because of the transforming power of God in us!

Peacemakers Come from a Pure Heart (make the following comments while remaining on this slide.)

True peacemakers provide some of the greatest demonstrations of God's love on this planet! Will you be one of them?

We have already experienced how the Beatitude of a pure heart elevates the quality of our relationships to an entirely different dimension. God's spirit compels us to guard these relationships as precious jewels: pure, polished, and transparent at all times.

At times we might also be required to step into confrontational situations to help others discover and preserve peace in their lives. As peacemakers, we are God's persistent envoys for peace at all times. This challenge is daunting in our earthly environment and requires strong courage, faith, and wisdom that can originate only from God.

In Matthew 5:40-41, Jesus provided practical applications to that day, "If anyone wants to sue you, and take your shirt, give him your coat also. And he who forces you to go one mile, go with him two." In Jesus' time, the Roman soldier was a universally hated figure. He was a symbol of forced foreign rule over the Hebrews' sovereign and God-sired nation. Under Roman law, any soldier had the right to compel a Jew to carry his armor or belongings the distance of one mile. Imagine the reaction of that soldier, accustomed to stubborn resistance and constant complaining, if he were asked after the first mile, "Sir, may I assist you for another mile?" Surely, that soldier's mouth would drop open and he would inquire with amazement why this additional service was being offered.

Such an opportunity would open the door for the believer to discuss God's great love for all mankind, even this despised Roman soldier. What an unexpected path this circumstance could provide to announce God's love for someone of the world! Open opportunities for evangelism.

Our greatest peacemaking assignment is to witness for Christ in every opportunity, both in word and deed. Jesus specifically gave us this mission, to bring the lost to him. "Therefore go and make disciples of all nations, baptizing them in the name of the Father and of the Son and of the Holy Spirit and teaching them to obey everything I have commanded you. And surely I am with you always, to the very end of the age." Matthew 28:19-20 The primary emphasis of peacemaking is evangelism. Sharing and spreading the Word of Christ.

Peace is love personified and is the true distinguishing mark of any follower of Christ. In John 13:34-35, Jesus tells the disciples, "A new commandment I give you: Love one another. As I have loved you, so you must love one another. By this everyone will know that you are my disciples, if you love one another." This love is not to be jealously guarded and practiced only among believers, but rather must be an overflowing, crusading current that sweeps others into God's family.

Primary Peacemaking Tools

One of the primary resources God has given us for this purpose is the multiple fruit of the Spirit as described in Galatians 5:22-23 NASB. "But the fruit of the Spirit is love, joy, peace, patience, kindness, goodness, faithfulness, gentleness, and self-control; against such things there is no law." Indeed, if we were all to permit these virtues to control our daily walk, would there be a need for law? God deeply desires to incorporate this complete fruit in the heart of every believer because it so dramatically promotes peacemaking and insures the spiritual quality of our lives—his Spirit living in us. Challenge the members to memorize Galatians 5:22-23 and to earnestly ask God to incorporate these spiritual qualities into every moment of their walk in the world. Such fruit in our lives is only possible with the fervent surrender to the Holy Spirit in our lives.

How do we assimilate these traits into our daily lives? By more of God and less of "me" living. "He must increase, but I must decrease," cried John the Baptist in John 3:30 NASB. God will honor this simple and humble request, and he will daily fill every believer who makes this his heart's cry. Assure group members that this sincere prayer to begin each day will create a much different life than they can ever live on their own! Make this your prayer to begin every day.

God's increased presence within us empowers the practice of peacemaking, not in our strength but in the strength and direction of the Holy Spirit. Peacemakers must depend upon heavenly wisdom, not human logic, to identify solutions and provide counsel. James 3:17 describes such wisdom as "first of all pure; then peace-loving, considerate, submissive, merciful and fruitful, impartial, and sincere." Heavenly wisdom invokes the Beatitudes of mourning, meekness, righteousness, and mercy. Proverbs 16:21 NASB describes how wisdom opens doors to effective peacemaking. "The wise in heart will be called discerning, and sweetness of speech increases persuasiveness."

The pure in heart have attained these attributes and enjoy impressive credibility to serve as effective peacemakers for the Lord. The collective results of the Beatitudes produce valuable preparation for the saints who serve in his kingdom. A bumper sticker message that I recently saw echoes a basic peacemaking principle, saying, "Wag more. Bark less." A dog wags its tail with its heart. Our hearts determine our actions also. Reach out to others.

A Prime Example: Peacemaker Ministries

The organization called Peacemaker Ministries is based on this particular Beatitude and practices conflict resolution with groups inside and outside the church by applying the principles of peacemaking found in the Bible. In his book *The Peacemaker*, Ken Sande, founder of Peacemaker Ministers, offers a practical strategy for aspiring peacemakers. He recommends using the following four *Gs* to bring reconciliation to marriages, families, friendships, the workplace, schools, and the church and the effective defeat of conflict.

- **G**lorify God. Seek to bring him glory in every situation, making this your selfless and supreme objective. This was Christ's primary goal in his life, death, and resurrection. All that he did here on earth was "to the glory of God the Father" (Philippians 2:11).
- **G**et the log out of your own eye. Don't blame others, but instead ask yourself, what have I contributed to this conflict? Relate in total honesty and seek confession from each party. Doing so cultivates the terrain for reconciliation.
- **G**ently restore the relationship. Don't ignore the other person, don't pretend that the problem doesn't exist, and don't talk to everyone else about that person. Recognize that person as valued and indispensable to the solution of this problem. Without his or her participation in this process, no solution will be found. Ask God to provide the right opportunity for sincere conversation. Pray for the moving of hearts among all involved.
- **G**o and be reconciled. Earnestly seek reconciliation, trusting in the Spirit of God to lead, direct, and bring it to pass. When God is working in hearts, reconciliation is eagerly accomplished. The resolution is often an emotional time of rejoicing, restoring, and becoming right with one another and before God.

There is a fifth *G* that underscores all the others: the **G**ospel of Jesus Christ. The gospel is what motivates every authentic peacemaker. It guides, directs, and empowers us to live and to share with others the true foundation of peace in this world. Because bringing life in Christ to others is the most profound and lasting peace we can offer on this earth, this is our principle task as peacemakers. We are fulfilling Christ's purpose, and completing the "big picture," just like Joseph!

The Beatitude Moment for the Peacemakers

Let God lead you to his peacemaking task. Doing it, you'll get "peace bumps." Commit to the cause! Have the members of the group close their eyes and ask God to reveal to them how they can be used as his peacemakers.

I Am the Vine

Jesus said in John 15:5, "I am the vine; you are the branches. If you remain in me and I in you, you will bear much fruit; apart from me you can do nothing." Our peacemaking efforts depend entirely upon the vine working within us to provide the solid spiritual sustenance and guidance we require to extend ourselves to others. We must be spiritually sensitive to what God is doing all around us and allow him to use us as he desires. If we don't pray daily for such sensitivity, we will be unused vessels in his kingdom. We must be branches extending to others!

We become his branches as we offer the shade of consolation and the fruit of reconciliation to others. We are only the conduits of peacemaking. Only Jesus can transform lives and reconcile broken relationships. Jesus, acting through us as the life-sustaining vine, will accomplish miracles. As peacemakers, we must be aware that God is constantly at work in people's lives, inching them toward himself. We must let him use us to entwine others into his kingdom and lead them to a peace that surpasses all understanding and supplies true consolation.

Some people need our support to help them stand. Others need our assistance to help bind them together. The estranged seek reconciliation. We must lead each of them first to the vine. Then we, as God's branches, can support, bind, and entwine as he uses us to intercede in each situation and help bring unity.

In Christ's vineyard, opportunities for peacemaking abound. Peace open doors. Peace take teamwork. Peace is God's golden egg. I leave peaceprints, wherever I go.

God's peace now resides powerfully in us. We are his peace, and a piece of him in this world. We must be makers and promoters of peace with all whom we encounter.

Peacemakers live a life "Beyond Belief"!

Thoughts for Meditation

- What peacemaking assignment has God given you?
- How are you promoting peace in your daily life?

Prayer for Peacemakers from Luke 6:35

"But love your enemies, do good to them that hate you, and lend to them without expecting to get anything back. Then your reward will be great, and you will be sons of the Most High, because he is kind to the ungrateful and wicked."

Peacemaking is the primary purpose in my life!

- Find His Burning Heart ......
- Play Beatitude song, *"Vessel of Peace" sung by Babbie Mason*

BEing the Beatitudes

After intensely praying to God about how he desires to use you as a peacemaker, write about how you feel him leading you to be a more active witness for him and/or involved or to take the initiative in a peacemaking mission. Follow his prompting to be used. Reflect on the verses following this chapter and recite by memory all the Beatitudes studied thus far.

Blessed are those who are persecuted for righteousness' sake, for theirs is the kingdom of heaven (Matthew 5:10)

Have the group read together this last Beatitude.

Where will effective peacemaking lead us? Peacemaking for God will provoke persecution in this world. Effective difference makers for God should anticipate negative reactions to their positive actions and false accusations in response to their good intentions.

The world is filled with and full of opposition from Satan. While the world chooses to reject the truth that Jesus is the only way to the Father, we who have experienced him know that he is all life, and life in abundance.

Yes, identity with Jesus in this world reaps persecution, and this is what every believer should expect and be ready to accept—not with fear, but confidence in Our Lord.

Ask group members what types of persecution for following God they have seen, read about, or experienced.

Let's consider the life Jesus lived that brought him to the cross. His sole objective was to follow God's specific direction each and every day.

- He manifested God's love wherever he was and to everyone around him.
- He stood up against evil and any opposition to God's commandments.
- He daily instructed his followers, showing them his way to live and to minister to others.

- He was constantly prepared for worldly reactions to his Godly actions. The Hebrew religious leaders, the Pharisees and Sadducees, never understood nor accepted Jesus as the true Messiah.

Jesus' worst moment on earth is described in pages 130-132 of the book. His most significant and challenging Beatitude moment here in this world was when his Father had no choice than to turn his back to his only son, because when the sin of the world descended upon him, the Father could not allow the presence of this sin to come before him! The continuous and treasured daily companionship that Jesus deeply experienced with his Father was suddenly ended on earth at the precise time of his most excruciating moment of his life! His Father was no longer "there" for him!

Show "How Love Wins" by Steven Curtis Chapman from *The Story* (music video is the next slide).

Expect Persecution

Much persecution exists in this evil world. Entire masses of humanity endure great wrongs; however, what separates the persecution of the blessed from the unjust suffering of others is the cause—for righteousness' sake. The blessed are persecuted because they refuse to renounce the sacred place of God in their lives.

John Gill explains that righteousness is a "righteous cause" for Christ and his gospel. It is actively professing Christ, showing an intense concern for his interest, and engaging in the defense of his person and truths. They "expose themselves to the rage and persecution of men." The gospel is not of man, "nor agreeable to the carnal reason of man," which is opposite to the way of faith. Men naturally refuse the way of faith because it excludes prideful boasting and is contrary to "carnal and selfish principles." Persecution will be by "the tongue, by cruel mockings, by repression, banishment, imprisonment, and innumerable sorts of death."

Gill continues, "but the saints, though thus used, or rather abused, are happy" for "theirs is the kingdom of heaven," and they enjoy the same blessedness as is pronounced for the "poor in spirit."

True spiritual joy is proclaiming the name of Jesus, his gospel, and entering eternal life with him. Here we see pictures of modern day martyrs' faith from World War II, Werner Betrand Bonhoffer, Richard Wurnbrand, and Corrie Tin Boom.

This last Beatitude instructs us to anticipate the same treatment in this world that Jesus experienced. Man, with his intolerance and unbelief, has not changed, nor has Satan. Righteousness refuses to renounce Christ. The God in us shines through to others as we offer tender mercy, maintain pure relationships, and pursue peace with all around us.

In the first century, persecution of the newly formed church was brutal and relentless. Satan and his world were cruelly attacking Christianity in every way possible. Paul exhorted his fellow believers, saying, "What, then, shall we say in response to these things? If God is for us, who can be against us? He who did not spare his own Son, but gave him up for us all—how will he not also, along with him, graciously give us all things? . . . Who shall separate us from the love of Christ? Shall trouble or hardship or persecution or famine or nakedness or danger or sword? As it is written: For your sake we face death all day long; we are considered as sheep to be slaughtered" (Romans 8:31-32, 35-36).

Martyrs are not only those who suffer death for Christ, but also those who live in a constant state of readiness to sacrifice their lives for his cause. God knows our hearts and how ready we are at any moment to pay the supreme price.

Righteous Living Like Jesus

Righteous living affects almost every waking decision. How will you begin your day—by clicking on the news or by seeking communion with the Lord of the universe? As you travel to school or to work, will you listen to the morning radio shows with their innuendos and their criticisms of others or tune to music or messages that will inspire you and focus you on Jesus for the day? During the day do you participate in gossip, or do you edify those around you? Do you plunge right into your midday meal or offer a word of grace while others stare or take note? Do you respond to a frustrating person with irritation and pride, or do you offer the offender grace and/or words of forgiveness? The daily choices are endless, but these decision points clearly display how sincerely we live for God.

Our decisions and actions for God predispose us to persecution by the world. What is our reaction to those individuals who seek to control us or who unexpectedly attack us? Do such instances reveal the presence of his Spirit within us and our daily spiritual discipline to demonstrate that we are followers of Christ?

Are we prepared to live as daily martyrs for Christ? To do so requires a deep denial of self. But just as Paul exhorts, such selflessness will cause others to ask for a defense of the gospel, opening the door to share why we are compelled and empowered to be different. What matters to others is not important to us; our only desire is to please God.

"Lord, into Your Hands I commend my spirit and my reputation" (T. W. Hunt and Claude N. King, *The Mind of Christ*).

Joshua 1:9 states, "Have I not commanded you? Be strong and courageous! Do not tremble or be dismayed, for the Lord your God is with you wherever you go." This is our promise from our God. We will never be alone or without him, regardless of what is happening to us as we follow him. We are his agents of change in an evil and rebellious world.

This final Beatitude does not demand that we be purposefully different, but that no matter what, we delight in living for Christ in every moment. This in itself will mark us as not of this world and will bring persecution our way. But persecution cannot derail us from a purposeful life in Christ. We must allow our adversaries to make us better, not bitter. This will only magnify God's presence in us as we resist the entangling snares of the Evil One. In martyrdom for Christ, our daily persecutions are small steps that eventually lead to longer strides.

Consider again the early church. Rome, in its power and pride, was out to destroy anything contrary to its gods and religious system in which the emperor was worshipped as a god. Christians would not bow down to these royal edicts, and so they expected persecution that would result in death. They considered it a privilege to carry their witness to this sacrificial stage. Every one of the apostles experienced such a death with the exception of John. Even though he was sentenced by the Romans to the island of Patmos to die of hard labor, but he survived to an advanced age.

Polycarp

Stories of supreme martyrdom were numerous during this early age of the church, and such was the final episode in the life of Polycarp. He was one of John's most dedicated disciples and served as bishop of the church in Smyrna during the latter years of his life. Tim LaHaye and Jerry B. Jenkins share the legend of Polycarp's death in *John's Story: The Last Eyewitness*.

Optional: have three people prepare to read this section in the roles of the Narrator, Polycarp, and the Roman Judge. Script is available in the Dropbox folder. (Slides accompany this script in the PowerPoint presentation.)

Narrator: When Polycarp was arrested he warmly greeted the Roman soldiers and offered them food. They granted his request to pray before they hauled him to Rome, and for two hours he prayed aloud. Many of the soldiers repented.

Facing death in the Coliseum, Polycarp was urged by one of the judges to renounce his faith and save himself.

"Reverence thy old age," the judge said. "Swear by Caesar's Fortune . . . and I will set thee at liberty. Reproach Christ!"

Polycarp responded, "Eighty and six years have I now served Christ, and he has never done me the least wrong: how can I blaspheme my King and Savior?"

The judge said, "I have wild beasts ready; to those I will cast you unless you repent."

"Call for them then," Polycarp said. "For we Christians are fixed in our minds not to change from good to evil; but for me it will be good to be changed from evil to good."

Furious, the judge said, "Seeing that you despise the wild beasts, I will cause you to be devoured by fire unless you repent."

Polycarp responded, "You threaten me with fire, which burns for an hour and then is extinguished; but do you not know of the fire of the future judgment of that eternal punishment which is reserved for the ungodly? But why tarry? Bring forth what you will!"

They took Polycarp to the stake to nail him there, but he said, "He who has given me strength to endure the fire will also enable me, without your securing me by nails, to stand without moving in the pile."

So he was merely tied to the stake. After Polycarp had prayed and thanked God for "bringing me to this day, and to this hour; that I should have a part in the number of your martyrs."

The executioner lit the fire. However, the flames arched around Polycarp like a sail of a ship, and he would not burn.

Finally the executioner was commanded to stab him with a sword. So much blood flowed that it extinguished the fire.

The fire had to be rekindled to burn Polycarp's body to ashes.

Although part of this story is obviously legend, the message is still powerful. Polycarp was eager and willing to die for our Lord, regardless of the pain associated with his death. God received the glory from his death and those of all martyrs throughout the generations. But martyrdom is not relegated to the past. It is pertinent now. Jesus said in Matthew 11:6, "Blessed is the man who does not fall away on account of me."

The Precipices of the Persecuted: We Are Martyrs Daily for Christ!

Our pathway has become a narrow ledge, but we risk it gladly to follow our Savior wherever he leads us. Whether our persecution is found in the daily denials of spiritual living or requires the surrender of life, the motivation and commitment are the same. This Beatitude is all about renouncing this world and getting closer to heaven

As peacemakers, we are equipped, ready, and eager to do whatever is necessary to proclaim Christ in this world. We can do nothing less. Our peacemaking has propelled us to this plane of living, and whether we die in a single physical act or daily in pieces, it is all for him. We are to be crusaders and heroes for Christ!

Discuss the slide "Degrees of Religious Persecution" from the powerpoint.

Play the video "Hero" by Kutless (music video is on the next slide).

Show the video from Voices of the Martyrs, "Liena's Prayer" about the suffering and persecution of Christians in Syria and her mindset to become a martyr if God wills it.

The Beatitude Moment for the Persecuted

Ask the members what ideas from this Beatitude have affected their thinking the most. Are they ready to live as martyrs for Christ?—putting themselves on the line in their witness for the Lord and daily making a difference for him? Now lead group members to come before God and ask themselves, "Am I ready to be persecuted for Christ, whether it be daily in pieces or all at once? What would be my reaction if such a situation presented itself to me?" After the prayer time, let group members share with one another their responses to these questions.

Be preoccupied with Christ and his purposes, not with the world's perception of you. Be prepared to plainly identify with and suffer for him in this world.

Thoughts for meditation

- Have you thanked God for any persecution experienced today for his cause?
- How is God preparing you to be more his martyr each day?

Find His Burning Heart …

Play the Beatitudes song, *"Persecution Proves Our Love for You" sung by Glass Temple.*

Closing prayer from Hebrews 12:1-3

Gather the members in a circle and lead them in the following prayer for the persecuted from Hebrews 12:1-3.

"Therefore, since we have so great a cloud of witnesses surrounding us, let us also lay aside every encumbrance, and the sin which so easily entangles us, and let us run with endurance the race that is set before us, fixing our eyes on Jesus, the author and perfecter of our faith, who, for the joy set before him, endured the cross, despising the shame, and has sat down at the right hand of the throne of God. For consider him who has endured such hostility by sinners against himself, so that you might not grow weary and lose heart."

BEing the Beatitudes

Reflect on the verses following this chapter. Recite all the Beatitudes as one complete passage. Consider your Beatitudes journey and where the Lord has led you on this quest and for what he is preparing you.

Conclusion

The Beatitudes are not won once and forever. They are God's permanent character infused in us. We, as humans, will still fall, fail, and flounder. The Beatitudes will define our lives, our passion, and our commitment to live out God's purpose in us.

They will keep us strong, spiritually robust, and ready to handle the challenges that will confront us in life. They will enable us to live life to the fullest with our God and in His Kingdom on earth. Our quest is far from over; in fact, it has only begun.

Continue to revisit the Beatitudes again and again to allow their truth and vigor to replenish and sweeten your continuing pilgrimage with our Lord until you reach the end, which is really just the beginning in eternity.

Play "All We Need" by Charlie Hall (audio on this slide).

Remember that Jesus is the great "I AM" and centerpiece of each Beatitude will give us a center of peace as we assimilate these spiritual treasures from him.

The Beatitudes in Couplets

As I concluded the book on the Beatitudes, and after having recited them countless times, I realized that they go together in pairs, and this also makes them easier to remember, regarding their purpose in us.

Forget Your Past—Leave Sin and Sorrow Behind

Blessed are the poor in spirit, for theirs is the kingdom of God. To experience salvation, we must sacrifice our human pride and any since of spiritual accomplishment that earns us salvation. We can only enter a sincere relationship with God after we grasp how holy and mighty he is and how unworthy, impure, and undeserving we are. God's all-surpassing greatness must occupy the center stage of our lives. Jesus said, "I am the door and anyone who enters by me will be saved." We are spiritual beggars, and the sole possession we carry into the Land of the Beatitudes is the cross of Christ. As we depart on this quest, we leave in his hands all our past sins and any spiritual pride that besets us. Our poverty is self, yet great spiritual riches await us as we set out in the vast Land of the Beatitudes.

Recognize Our Lord for all he is, and our desperate and destitute position before him.

Blessed are those who mourn, for they will be comforted. When life's tragedies assault us, we must turn to God for his all-surpassing grace, strength, and peace, which exceed human comprehension. Jesus said in John 4:14 NASB, "Whoever drinks of the water that I will give him will never thirst." Jesus is our well, and only his soul-saturating comfort can enable us to leave our mourning behind for the morning of a new day. The deep message of this Beatitude is our total dependence on God every single day in every personal need and in every circumstance we encounter. As partakers of this heavenly comfort, we must to extend to others the comfort of Christ as prayerful intercessors for those who are hurting.

Turn all your burdens over to Christ and depend totally on him every day.

Focus First on God—Forget Self and Feast on the Word

Blessed are the meek, for they will inherit the earth. As believers in Christ, we are not of this world. Our zeal must be for the heavenly realm where our true citizenship resides. Jesus said in John 8:12 NASB, "I am the light of the world . . . he who walks in me will have the light of life." We no longer serve ourselves. We have put the "mighty me" in the back seat, and the light of Jesus and his gentle strength have become clearly visible in us. No earthly or selfish distraction can deter us from our heavenly purpose as we live with a "turn the cheek" mentality. Our great joy is to allow Christ to consume us more each day. His brilliance increases as our light diminishes.

Give Christ the preeminent position in your life.

Blessed are those who hunger and thirst for righteousness, for they will be filled. We have eliminated the primary spiritual distractions in life: spiritual pride, burdens weighing us down, and our dominating self. As we forget the past and focus on God, we develop a ravenous appetite for the delicacies of his Word. Scrumptious morsels await each believer! As we immerse ourselves daily and more deeply in his Word, we will desire it more and God will fill us to overflowing. Jesus said in John 6:48, "I am the bread of life." We dine daily on this bread, the written Word, while Jesus, the living Word, resides within us. Our hunger is for him to take us over in Word and in person.

Feast fully on the bountiful provisions of God's word and let it truly transform you.

Fellowship Fully with Your Lord—Fill Yourself with His Presence

Blessed are the merciful, for they will be shown mercy. We are mercy-filled by Christ and are specially equipped to resist the mercy-less attacks of this world, just as was our Savior. Jesus said in John 11:25, "I am the resurrection and the life . . . he who believes in me will live, even though he dies." His mercy resurrects our souls and compels us to share that same mercy with others. His mercy fills us and extends even to our most awful offenders. Mercy will conquer negative confrontations and open the door for God's unconditional love to astonish others. We must maintain his mercy-full mentality in every step of life, allowing God's Spirit to fill us, while his pardoning power is embedded in our being.

Allow his mercy to consume you with a fervent passion to forgive and reach out to others.

Blessed are the pure in heart, for they will see God. The pure in heart enjoy total harmony with God's heart and the closest communion possible. Jesus said in John 9:5, "While I am in the world, I am the light of the world." God's holy light now fully illuminates us. We have purged ourselves of any ungodliness. His purity within us harnesses our willpower to resist the enticing attractions of this world, empowers purity in our thought lives, motivations, and innermost desires. We are totally transparent before him and in our relationships with others. We clearly see him and his burden for our world. His heart resides on the throne of our lives. We will become his effective instruments. We discover true life and true purpose in Our Lord!

Be totally transparent before God as he transforms you toward his perfect purpose for your life!

Find His Burning Heart—and Let It Consume You

Blessed are the peacemakers, for they will be called sons of God. Peacemakers are God's diplomats on earth, consumed with a powerful passion to promote his peace, and primarily His Gospel. We are his children and implant his love in the lives of all those around us and are willing to confront conflict to reconcile people to him. Effective peacemaking is not accomplished through human effort, but only in the strength, leadership, and wisdom of the Lord. Jesus said in John 15:5, "I am the vine; you are the branches . . . apart from me you can do nothing." We branch out to others and bring them to Christ. God uses us to transform broken relationships and to push back the frontiers of evil in this world. Peacemaking demands courage and risk, but what mighty rewards result!

Become a soldier in this battle and plant the peace of the gospel in the lives of all around you.

Blessed are those who are persecuted because of righteousness' sake, for theirs is the kingdom of heaven. Our true identity is found in heaven, and we are set apart to be different in this world. Every day we are called to make a stand for Christ. Although our hearts are fixed toward the eternal, our feet are planted in earthly reality and we will confront earthly consequences for following our Lord. Persecution magnifies our witness on earth and glorifies our Father. Jesus proclaimed in John 14:6, "I am the way and the truth and the life. No one comes to the Father except through me." Just as the world persecuted Jesus for his declaration of himself, our world today will persecute us for our declaration of him! Be ready to bear all injustice, ridicule, and consequences to proclaim the Lord. The consuming fire of God's heart is burning in us to bring the whole world to him through Christ!

Be prepared for persecution as you proclaim Jesus Christ every single day.

May we strive to BEcome all we can in Christ, veterans of the Beatitudes, delighting in the closest communion possible with him, and being used as powerful in—all for him!

Group Game: **Match the Beatitude**. As the group members view each of the Land of the Beatitudes pictures (following in separate slides), have them tell which Beatitude the artwork represents and tell why that picture relates to this particular Beatitude.

The Purposeful Sequenced Order of the Beatitudes

Ask the group: Why are the Beatitudes sequenced as they are? Ask the members to share their insights about the purposeful order of the Beatitudes. Discuss how each one fully prepares us for the next. This is very important to understand.

Discussion Guide:

- **First three Beatitudes**

The poor in spirit: We cannot enter into a realistic and true relationship with God until we comprehend his greatness and grandeur and our spiritual poverty and insignificance in comparison with him. Yet, regardless of these infinite extremes, God seeks a personal relationship with each one of us, although we are merely destitute spiritual beggars before him. He yearns to fill us with his amazing spiritual riches.

Those who mourn: After we have encountered our supreme and caring Creator, how can we not turn over our problems and wearying burdens to him? When we decide to release our burdens to Christ and depend totally on him, the heavenly consolation of this Beatitude becomes a reality.

The meek: Once we transfer the weights of our world to Christ, we know that he can manage our lives infinitely better than the "mighty me" that strives to dominate our every decision. We put the "me" in the back seat and let Jesus become our designated driver.

- **The Next Three Beatitudes**

Those who hunger and thirst for righteousness' sake: We have set aside three major distractions for many believers: spiritual pride, emotional and spiritual burdens weighing us down, and an addictive preoccupation with self. Now our primary desire is to know and experience God more deeply every day. We dive into and dine upon his Word—the Written word of Scripture and the Living Word of Jesus living in us.

The merciful: Feasting on God's Word unlocks the deep expanses of his justice, mercy, and grace. His standard of justice is holy and perfect, his passionate mercy loves without exception, and his gift of grace offers salvation to all who will accept it. God's unconditional love becomes our mentality, animating all of our behavior.

The pure in heart: Our comprehension of God's vast mercy gives us confidence to open our hearts to his intimate scrutiny to reveal any secret, resistant, or unknown sin impeding a full relationship with our Lord. Confessing these sins releases us to become totally transparent with God. We see him and the world through his eyes. Our desire is to purify every relationship we have.

- **The Last Two Beatitudes**

The peacemakers: Our pure heart before God gives us the same view of the world as is Christ's, and his burden for the world becomes our burden. We are emissaries of his peace and ready for spiritual battle to promote that peace with all in our paths. His heart is our heart!

The persecuted: Effective peacemaking brings persecution in this world. We are prepared for the evil opposition that confronts us. Every aspect of our being is in harmony with God. Our only desire is to be with him.

Ask the group how helpful is it now to see how each of the Beatitudes leads us to and prepares us for the next one.

The Beatitude Mentalities

Each Beatitude attitude is a mentality that we acquire as we sincerely experience each one.

The poor in spirit: I recognize my spiritual poverty, which will result in heavenly riches.

Those who mourn: I release all my hurts and worries to the Lord.

The meek: I submit myself to him and turn the other cheek, never to be deterred from his will in my life.

Those who hunger and thirst for righteousness: I maintain a stay-hungry attitude and feast on God's Word.

The merciful: His mercy has filled me and I will let it flood others.

The pure in heart: I purify my heart to attain total transparency with God and all around me.

The peacemakers: I will be a vessel of God's peace on this earth to be used by him.

Those persecuted for righteousness' sake: I am ready and willing to give up everything anytime for him.

Concluding Questions to Reflect Upon and Discuss

1. Have the Beatitudes made you different from who you were before?
2. What major purposes in your life has God revealed to you in the Beatitudes?

• Next Question

Is God spiritually empowering your life now through:

• Intense daily communion with him?
• Daily intake of his Word?

- Daily searching and sensitivity to his workings in your life?
- Courage to make a daily difference for him?
- Becoming more beautiful in and for him?

- Next Question

Will you lead others through the Beatitudes quest? Don't you want your fellow believers to experience this "growing closer to Jesus and God" also?

Let the Beatitudes BEcome God's attitude in you. Be in full fellowship with him. Become the "who" he created you to be. Let the Beatitudes beautify you before God. Let him see his beauty in you! Become a hero and a difference-maker in this world as he changes you every day! His Spirit will become your beloved master and rule you more each day. Commit to the quest to be all that you were meant to be in Christ, because in the end, you'll be so glad you did!

Looking to our Future beyond this earth

Play "Already There" by Casting Crowns (music video on next slide).

Discuss how fantastic it will be to look back over your life from heaven and enjoy the view because you undertook the Beatitudes quest for our Lord.

Will you look back with Our Lord on the beauty of a Beatitudes life?

Play "Song of the Redeemed" by Charlie Hall (audio begins on this slide and continues through the slides with the lyrics). This is a great description of a Beatitudes believer's life on earth! Sing it together after hearing it once.

> We sing it in the darkest place
> 'Cause love is in Your powerful name. We shine the light of beauty and grace. We're living in the Name that can save.
> We sing to You the song of the redeemed.
> You beautified our hearts and made us clean.
> You've rescued us from death and set us free.
> We sing to You the song of the redeemed.
>
> We adore You, stand before You, Forgiven and redeemed.
> Come all races from all places.

Around the cross we sing.

We are Yours. We are Yours. We are Yours.

We are Yours. We are Yours. We are Yours.

View video *"Move in Me"* by Jeremy Camp (conversion of Saul) from The Story (music video on next slide).

May the Beatitudes greatly bless your life, and the lives of others.

Play the conclusion Beatitudes song, ***"The Beatitudes Are Your Beauty in Me" featuring Bucky Heard, Annette Heardon, David Staton, and Babbie Mason.***

Gather in a circle, recite the Beatitudes as a group, and pray together, thanking God for what he has revealed to participants through this study and for how the Beatitudes have made and will make their lives and walk with God delightfully different and powerfully purposeful for him!

THE BEATITUDES AND SCRIPTURE PASSAGES BY BEATITUDE

Memorize them!

Blessed are the poor in spirit, for theirs is the kingdom of heaven. Blessed are those who mourn, for they shall be comforted.

Blessed are the meek, for they shall inherit the earth.

Blessed are those who hunger and thirst after righteousness, for they shall be filled.

Blessed are the merciful, for they shall receive mercy. Blessed are the pure in heart, for they shall see God.

Blessed are the peacemakers, for they shall be called the children of God.

Blessed are those who are persecuted for righteousness sake, for theirs is the kingdom of heaven. (Matthew 5:3-10)

Blessed are the poor in spirit, for theirs is the kingdom of heaven.

His greatness:

"Many, O Lord my God, are the wonderful works which you have done, and your thoughts toward us; no one can compare with you! If I should declare and speak of them, they are too many to be numbered" (Psalm 40:5).

"All your works shall praise you, O Lord, and your loving ones shall bless you affectionately, and gratefully shall your saints confess and praise you! They shall speak of the glory of your kingdom and talk of your power. Who would not fear you, O king of the nations? For it is fitting to you and your due! For among all the wise of the nations and in all their kingdoms, there is none like you" (Jeremiah 10:6-7).

"From the rising of the sun to the going down of it and from east to west, the name of the Lord is to be praised!" (Psalm 113:3).

"Amen! they cried. Blessing and glory and majesty and splendor and wisdom and thanks and honor and power and might be ascribed to our God forever and ever, throughout the eternities of the eternities! Amen!" (Revelation 7:12).

Our spiritual poverty:

"Now thanks be to God for his gift, his indescribable, inexpressible, free gift!" (2 Corinthians 9:15).

"For your name's sake, O Lord, pardon my iniquity and my guilt, for they are great" (Psalm 25:11).

"Praised, honored, blessed be the God and Father of our Lord Jesus Christ! By his boundless mercy we have been born again to an ever-living hope through the resurrection of Jesus Christ from the dead, born anew into an inheritance which is beyond the reach of change and decay [imperishable], unsullied and unfading, reserved in heaven for you" (1 Peter 1:3-4).

Blessed are those who mourn, for they shall be comforted.

"Even though I walk through the darkest valley, I will fear no evil, for you are with me, your rod and your staff, they comfort me" (Psalm 23:4).

"The Lord is my rock, and my fortress, and my deliver. My God, my rock, in whom I take refuge. My shield and the horn of my salvation, my stronghold" (Psalm 18:2).

"Give me a sign of your goodness, that my enemies may see it and be put to shame, for you, Lord, have helped me and comforted me" (Psalm 86:17).

"Remember your word to your servant, for you have given me hope. My comfort in my suffering is this: Your promise preserves my life" (Psalm 119:49-50).

"May your unfailing love be my comfort, according to your promise to your servant" (Psalm 119:76).

"I will praise you, Lord. Although you were angry with me, your anger has turned away and you have comforted me" (Isaiah 12:1).

"Shout for joy, you heavens; rejoice, you earth; burst into song, you mountains! For the Lord comforts his people and will have compassion on his afflicted ones" (Isaiah 49:13).

"Do not let your hearts be troubled. You believe in God; believe also in me. My Father's house has many rooms; if that were not so, would I have told you that I am going there to prepare a place for you? And if I go and prepare a place for you, I will come back and take you to be with me that you also may be where I am" (John 14:1-3).

Blessed are the meek, for they shall inherit the earth.

"In his distress he sought the favor of the Lord his God and humbled himself greatly before the God of his ancestors" (2 Chronicles 33:12).

"Your beginnings will seem humble, so prosperous will your future be" (Job 8:7). "He guides the humble in what is right and teaches them his way" (Psalm 25:9). "For the Lord delights in his people; he crowns the humble with victory" (Psalm 149:4).

"Once more the humble will rejoice in the Lord; the needy will rejoice in the Holy One of Israel" (Isaiah 29:19).

"For those who exalt themselves will be humbled, and those who humble themselves will be exalted" (Matthew 23:12).

"Be completely humble and gentle; be patient, bearing with one another in love" (Ephesians 4:2).

"Humble yourselves in the presence of the Lord, and he will lift you up" (James 4:10).

"Humble yourselves, therefore, under God's mighty hand, that he might lift you up in due time" (1 Peter 5:6).

"Finally, all of you, be like-minded, be sympathetic, love one another, be compassionate and humble. Do not repay evil with evil or insult with insult. On the contrary, repay evil with blessing, because to this you were called so that you may inherit a blessing" (1 Peter 3:8-9).

Blessed are those who hunger and thirst after righteousness, for they shall be filled.

"The Law of the Lord is perfect, restoring the soul; the testimony of the Lord is sure, making wise the simple. The precepts of the Lord are right, rejoicing the heart; the commandment of the Lord is pure, enlightening the eyes. The fear of the Lord is clean, enduring forever. The judgments of the Lord are true; they are righteous altogether. They are more desirable than gold, yes, than much fine gold, sweeter than honey and the drippings of the honeycomb. Moreover, by them thy servant is warned; in keeping them there is great reward" (Psalm 19:7-11).

"The Lord loves righteousness and justice; the earth is full of his unfailing love" (Psalm 33:5).

"My mouth shall tell of thy righteousness, and of thy salvation, all the day long; for I do not know the sum of them. I will come with the mighty deeds of the Lord God; I will make mention of thy righteousness, thine alone" (Psalm 71:15-16).

"Faithfulness springs forth from the earth, and righteousness looks down from heaven" (Psalm 85:11).

"Thy Word is a lamp to my feet, and a light to my path" (Psalm 119:105).

Other verses concerning righteousness:

"If anyone loves me, he will keep my word; and my Father will love him, and we will come to him, and make our abode with him" (John 14:23).

"God made him who had no sin to be sin for us, so that in him we might become the righteousness of God" (2 Corinthians 5:21).

"I do not set aside the grace of God, for if righteousness could be gained through the law, Christ died for nothing!" (Galatians 2:21).

"All Scripture is God-breathed and is useful for teaching, rebuking, correcting, and training in righteousness, that the man of God may be adequate, equipped for every good work" (2 Timothy 3:16-17).

"Now there is in store for me the crown of righteousness, which the Lord, the righteous judge, will award to me on that day—and not only to me, but also to all who have longed for his appearing" (2 Timothy 4:8).

Blessed are the merciful, for they shall receive mercy.

"And the Lord said, 'I will cause all my goodness to pass in front of you, and I will proclaim my name, the Lord, in your presence. I will have mercy on whom I will have mercy, and I will have compassion on whom I will have compassion'" (Exodus 33:19). "David said to God, 'I am in deep distress. Let me fall into the hands of the Lord, for his mercy is very great; but do not let me fall into human hands'" (1 Chronicles 21:13).

"But go and learn what this means: 'I desire mercy, not sacrifice.' For I have not come to call the righteous, but sinners" (Matthew 9:13).

"Whoever conceals their sins does not prosper, but the one who confesses and renounces them finds mercy" (Proverbs 28:13).

"What then shall we say? Is God unjust? Not at all! For he says to Moses, 'I will have mercy on whom I have mercy, and I will have compassion on whom I have compassion.' It does not, therefore, depend on human desire or effort, but on God's mercy" (Romans 9:14-16).

"All of us also lived among them at one time, gratifying the cravings of our flesh and following its desires and thoughts. Like the rest, we were by nature deserving of wrath. But because of his great love for us, God, who is rich in mercy, made us alive with Christ even when we were dead in transgressions—it is by grace you have been saved" (Ephesians 2:3-5).

"Remember, Lord, your great mercy and love, for they are from of old" (Psalm 25:6).

"Have mercy on me, O God, according to your unfailing love; according to your great compassion blot out my transgressions" (Psalm 51:1).

"For I desire mercy, not sacrifice, and acknowledgment of God rather than burnt offerings" (Hosea 6:6).

"For God has bound everyone over to disobedience so that he may have mercy on them all" (Romans 11:32).

"He has shown you, O man, what is good. And what does the Lord require of you?

To act justly and to love mercy and to walk humbly with your God" (Micah 6:8). "But the tax collector stood at a distance. He would not even look up to heaven, but beat his breast and said, 'God, have mercy on me, a sinner'" (Luke 18:13).

"Jesus said, 'Go home to your own people and tell them how much the Lord has done for you, and how he has had mercy on you'" (Mark 5:19).

"If it is to encourage, then give encouragement; if it is giving, then give generously; if it is to lead, do it diligently; if it is to show mercy, do it cheerfully" (Romans 12:8).

"Because judgment without mercy will be shown to anyone who has not been merciful. Mercy triumphs over judgment" (James 2:13).

"But the wisdom that comes from heaven is first of all pure; then peaceloving, considerate, submissive, full of mercy and good fruit, impartial and sincere" (James 3:17).

"Praise be to the God and Father of our Lord Jesus Christ! In his great mercy he has given us new birth into a living hope through the resurrection of Jesus Christ from the dead" (1 Peter 1:3).

"Mercy, peace, and love be yours in abundance" (Jude 1:2).

Blessed are the pure in heart, for they shall see God.

"Create in me a pure heart, O God, and renew a steadfast spirit within me" (Psalm 51:10).

"Search me, O Lord, and know my heart; try me and know my anxious thoughts; and see if there is any hurtful way within me, and lead me in the everlasting way" (Psalm 139:23-24).

"Flee the evil desires of youth and pursue righteousness, faith, love, and peace, along with those who call on the Lord out of a pure heart" (2 Timothy 2:22).

"Let us draw near to God with a sincere heart and with the full assurance that faith brings, having our hearts sprinkled to cleanse us from a guilty conscience and having our bodies washed with pure water" (Hebrews 10:22).

Blessed are the peacemakers, for they shall be called the children of God.

"For the kingdom of God is not a matter of eating and drinking, but of righteousness, peace, and joy in the Holy Spirit" (Romans 14:17).

"Make every effort to live in peace with all men and to be holy; without holiness no one will see the Lord" (Hebrews 12:14).

"Let us therefore make every effort to do what leads to peace and to mutual edification" (Romans 14:19).

"Peacemakers who sow in peace raise a harvest of righteousness" (James 3:18).

"If it is possible, as far as it depends on you, live at peace with everyone" (Romans 12:18).

"My dear brothers, take note of this: Everyone should be quick to listen, slow to speak and slow to become angry, for man's anger does not bring about the righteous life that God desires" (James 1:19-20).

"Aim for perfection, listen to my appeal, be of one mind, and live in peace. And the God of love and peace will be with you" (2 Corinthians 13:11).

"Bear with each other and forgive whatever grievances you may have against one another. Forgive as the Lord forgave you" (Colossians 13:3).

"For God was pleased to have all his fullness dwell in him, and through him to reconcile to himself all things, whether things on earth or things in heaven, by making peace through his blood shed on the cross" (Colossians 1:19-20).

Blessed are those who are persecuted for righteousness' sake, for theirs is the kingdom of heaven.

"We are hard pressed on every side, but not crushed; perplexed, but not in despair; persecuted, but not abandoned; struck down, but not destroyed. We always carry around in our body the death of Jesus, so that the life of Jesus may also be revealed in our body" (2 Corinthians 4:8-10).

"But even if I am being poured out as a drink offering upon the sacrifice and service of your faith, I rejoice and share my joy with you all" (Philippians 2:17-18).

"Remember what I told you: 'A servant is not greater than his master.' If they persecuted me, they will persecute you also. If they obeyed my teaching, they will obey yours also" (John 15:20).

"Then you will be handed over to be persecuted and put to death, and you will be hated by all nations because of me" (Matthew 24:9).

"At that time the son born according to the flesh persecuted the son born by the power of the Spirit. It is the same now" (Galatians 4:29).

"In fact, everyone who wants to live a godly life in Christ Jesus will be persecuted" (2 Timothy 3:13).

"If we live, we live for the Lord; and if we die, we die for the Lord. So, whether we live or die, we belong to the Lord" (Romans 14:8).

"Rejoice and be glad, for your reward in heaven is great, for so they persecuted the prophets who were before you" (Matthew 5:12).

"We work hard with our own hands. When we are cursed, we bless; when we are persecuted, we endure it" (1 Corinthians 4:12).

"All your commands are trustworthy; help me, for I am being persecuted without cause" (Psalm 119:86)

"To this you were called, because Christ suffered for you, leaving you an example, that you should follow in his steps" (1 Peter 2:21).

THE BEATITUDES BIBLE STUDY PARTICIPANT GUIDE

This participant's guide has been prepared to assist the readers of Marlin Harris' book, *Let the Beatitudes Be the Attitude in You* published by West Bow Press in 2012, to engage both the book, and more importantly, the text of Scripture known as the Beatitudes.

The guide includes questions that are designed to help the reader interact with each section of the book, and in turn to enhance group discussions. There are two types of questions: (1) Fact questions are intended to help the reader focus on the information in the chapter or section of the book and the Scripture. Answering them is a matter of simply writing down what the book says! (2) Application/Discussion questions will ask the reader to think about the information studied and to relate that information to life.

These questions may easily provoke more questions, differing opinions, and creative solutions among group participants. In your discussions, remember not only Jesus' words in the Beatitudes, "Blessed are the peacemakers, for they will be called the sons of God," but also the Apostle Paul's words to the Church at Ephesus, "*Let no corrupting talk come out of your mouths, but only such as is good for building up, as fits the occasion, that it may give grace to those who hear.*" (Eph 4:29 ESV) After all, what are the Beatitudes but purveyors of God's grace!

Dr. Ray H. Cureton is a Presbyterian Church in America ordained minister with 17 years pastoral ministry experience. Dr. Cureton also retired from the USAF after 20 years where he served as a Security Policeman and an Air Force Recruiter. Dr. Cureton recieved a Bachelor of Arts degree (1984), a Master of Divinity (1998), and a Doctor of Ministry in Pastoral Leadership (2012) from Columbia International University, Columbia, SC. He is married to the former Silvana S. DiPaolo of Paris France. The Curetons have 2 children and 7 grandchildren.

Please begin your study by reading through the
Beatitudes from Matthew 5:1-12 –

1. NOW WHEN JESUS SAW THE CROWDS, HE WENT UP ON A MOUNTAINSIDE AND SAT DOWN. HIS DISCIPLES CAME TO HIM.

2. AND HE BEGAN TO TEACH THEM.

3. "BLESSED ARE THE POOR IN SPIRIT, FOR THEIRS IS THE KINGDOM OF HEAVEN.

4. "BLESSED ARE THOSE WHO MOURN, FOR THEY WILL BE COMFORTED.

5. "BLESSED ARE THE MEEK, FOR THEY WILL INHERIT THE EARTH.

6. "BLESSED ARE THOSE WHO HUNGER AND THIRST FOR RIGHTEOUSNESS, FOR THEY WILL BE FILLED.

7. "BLESSED ARE THE MERCIFUL, FOR THEY WILL BE SHOWN MERCY.

8. "BLESSED ARE THE PURE IN HEART, FOR THEY WILL SEE GOD.

9. "BLESSED ARE THE PEACEMAKERS, FOR THEY WILL BE CALLED CHILDREN OF GOD.

10. "BLESSED ARE THOSE WHO ARE PERSECUTED BECAUSE OF RIGHTEOUSNESS, FOR THEIRS IS THE KINGDOM OF HEAVEN.

11. "BLESSED ARE YOU WHEN PEOPLE INSULT YOU, PERSECUTE YOU AND FALSELY SAY ALL KINDS OF EVIL AGAINST YOU BECAUSE OF ME.

12. REJOICE AND BE GLAD, BECAUSE GREAT IS YOUR REWARD IN HEAVEN, FOR IN THE SAME WAY THEY PERSECUTED THE PROPHETS WHO WERE BEFORE YOU.

Preliminaries – Pages xxi-xxxii

Fact Questions

1. According to the author, what "potential" do the beatitudes "possess?"(See pg. xxiii). *"To spiritually transform God's people."* (pg. xxiii)

2. Mr. Harris writes, "The beatitudes must be experienced personally…" What does he say will be the collective result of such personal experience? (see pg. xxiii) *It "will unify, edify, equip, and dynamically direct his body into the great purpose of salvation for the world to gain glory for the Father." (pg. xxiii)*

3. What is Jesus' "deep desire for us?" *"To find profound happiness, contentment, fulfillment, and confidence in our walk with him." (pg. xxiii.)*

4. What is "true blessedness on this earth?" (see pg. xxiii) *"Being one with God and seizing his victorious attitude in this life."(pg. xxiii)*

5. According to the author, the Beatitudes are God's "great design to bring us boundless blessings." What does Mr. Harris say is the "only" way we can find such blessings? (See pg. xxiv). *"Only as we move closer to God." (pg. xxiv.)*

6. Who or what does the author call the "centerpiece of the Beatitudes?" (See pg. xxvii). *Jesus Christ (pg. xxvii)*

7. T/F _____ The author believes the Beatitudes demonstrate that what we do is more important than what we are. (See pg. xxviii). *False. Just the opposite is true – what we are is more important than what we do.*

8. With what do each of the Beatitudes begin and end according to the author? (See pg. xxviii). *The heart (pg. xxviii)*

Application/Discussion Questions

Application Question #1: Review fact question 1. Do you agree that the Beatitudes have the potential to spiritually transform God's people? Why or why not?

Application Question #2: Review fact question 2. What do you think it means to "experience" the beatitudes personally? Give an example of how you personally have experienced the Beatitudes.

Application Question #3: Review fact question 3. On a scale of 1-5 with 5 being the highest, rate the "happiness, contentment, fulfillment, and confidence" you have in your walk with Jesus Christ as you start this study. How do you think studying the Beatitudes might raise your answer?

Application Question #4: Review fact question 5. How "close" does one have to be to God to "receive" the blessings? How will you know when you have done enough to get close enough to receive those blessings?

Application Question #5: Review fact question 6. In what way or ways do you believe Jesus is the 'centerpiece' of the Beatitudes?

Application Question #6: Review fact question 7. Do you agree with Mr. Harris? Explain why what you are is more important than what you do.

Application Question #7: Review fact question 8. Describe what you understand the heart to refer to in Scripture.

Application Question #8: In the prologue, Marlin Harris strongly advises the reader of the need to enter a quest using the Beatitudes. What do you understand to be the purpose of this quest and what it will take to complete it?

Chapter 1 – *"God's Heart Language"* – Pages 1-6

Fact Questions

1. What does *"a heart language"* provide between two beings? (See pg. 1). *"The deepest level of communication."* *(pg. 1)*

2. What *"is effortlessly shared"* in this heart language? (See pg. 1). *"Profound emotions, direct meanings, and precise ideas."*

3. What does the Guarani word *angaipa* illustrate about our heart condition? (See pg. 2) *It unlocks "the exact idea of sin: filth, degradation, and depravity." (pg. 2)*

4. What is the "primary purpose of our salvation gift from God?" (See pg. 2-3) *"To reestablish that original, true, and full fellowship with him that was lost in the garden of Eden…due to the sinful fall of man." (pg. 2-3)*

5. What "aim" does the author believe the Beatitudes will help the believer attain, and what will it take to achieve a "heavenly mind set?" (See pg. 3) *"To pursue the deepest personal experience possible with him." Our pursuit of this heavenly mindset "must be relentless and sincere." (pg. 3)*

6. How does A.T. Robertson describe the concept of "blessed" in the Beatitudes? (See pg. 4) *"The simple idea of happy was 'ennobled' and transformed by Jesus to indicate an inner, deeply seated contentment evident of pure character and motivation that is not subject to outward circumstances, but is inward in its origin." (pg. 4)*

7. Why does Harris believe Jesus pronounced the Beatitude blessings at the beginning of the Sermon on the Mount? (See pg. 4). *"To prepare hearts for what he had yet to say in the Sermon on the Mount. . . . A Beatitudes heart could better comprehend his Sermon's profound spiritual truths and more easily employ them in daily thought and deed."(pg. 4)*

8. What is the "source and lamp of spiritual insight" and what does the author advise you to do with it? (See pg. 4). *God's Holy Word, and he wants you to both "savor" and memorize it.*

9. What does the author say the Beatitudes will remove from you? (See pg. 5) *"Some unholy and distasteful part of you, according to God's holy standard, and will replace it with something much more fulfilling and significant." (Pg. 5)*

10. What does Mr. Harris say must, "drive us daily?" (See pg. 5). *"An earnest and deep determination to know God." (pg. 5)*

BEFORE GOING ON TO THE APPLICATION/DISCUSSION QUESTIONS BELOW LET ME ENCOURAGE YOU TO LOOK FOR A 'BEATITUDE MOMENT' AS YOU MEDITATE ON EACH CHAPTER TO FOLLOW. WHAT IS A 'BEATITUDE MOMENT?' PERHAPS IT IS A CONVICTION OF OUR SIN AND FAILINGS, OR A REALIZATION THAT GOD IN CHRIST IS THE EMBODIMENT OF THAT PARTICULAR BEATITUDE THAT OVERCOMES THAT SIN IN YOUR LIFE; AND HOPEFULLY IT WILL BE BOTH!

Application/Discussion Questions

Application Question #1: Review Fact questions 1-3. What is the basic heart language of the human condition and what problem does such a condition identify?

Application Question #2: Examine the *present* condition of your own heart. What areas of concern does this examination bring to the fore that the Beatitudes might help address?

Application Question #3: Review fact question 4. How (by what means) is full fellowship reestablished with God?

Application Question #4: Review fact question 8. What are some ways you have learned to 'savor' the Word of God?

Application Question #5: Review fact questions 9-10. Describe the commitment it will take for the Beatitudes, in the power of the Holy Spirit, to identify sin in your life and to replace that sin with God's own character.

Application Question #6: Answer the two "Thoughts for meditation" questions on page 6 of the book.

Chapter 2 – "The Poor in Spirit" – Pages 7-23

Fact Questions

11. Review Saul's conversion experience on pages 7-11. What did Saul need to "confront" before "God could take up residence in his heart?" (See pg. 11). *"[The] wretched reality of his own spiritual poverty." (pg. 11)*

12. According to Harris, if we are to experience Jesus as Paul did (though maybe not as dramatically), what will it take from us? (See pg. 11). *"Such an experience demands that we leave behind our personal itineraries, prideful identities, and unyielding ideas as to what we will accomplish in this life." (pg. 11)*

13. According to the book on page 11, what will God do in response to our surrender of these itineraries, identities, and ideas? (See pg. 11) *He "fills us with Himself and His purpose to make us useful instruments in His kingdom." (pg. 11)*

14. When did you avail yourself of the offer of salvation and, according to page 12, specifically, upon what is your salvation based? (See pg. 12) *Jesus is the door and only way of salvation having "paid the great sin sacrifice on the cross that each of us owed." (pg. 12)*

15. What did Jesus' death "unleash?" (See pg. 12) *"Unimaginable spiritual treasures for all who believe. (pg. 12)*

16. "Having achieved their objective of eternal security," what must people avoid? (See pg. 12) *Spiritual complacency and becoming "tenants in the land of lukewarmness."(pg. 12)*

17. What is our "sole possession as we enter the land of the Beatitudes?" (See pg. 14) *The cross. (pg. 14)*

18. Realizing that "God will accept nothing less than the confession of our desperate sinful state and a sincere profession of Jesus as our Savior," with what does our "remaking process in the Beatitudes" begin? (See pg. 14) *"The unearthing of our abject spiritual poverty." (pg. 14)*

19. T/F _____ According to the book, our worldly possessions are "essential assets in God's Kingdom." Explain your answer. (See pg. 14) *False – they are an "erroneous compass setting in God's spiritual realm." (pg. 14)*

20. According to Harris, what is the "degree of spiritual poverty we must recognize in ourselves?" (See pgs. 14-15) *It is "being totally destitute of wealth, influence, position, and honor, and being completely powerless to accomplish what one desires." (pg. 14-15)*

21. According to John Gill, those who "see their spiritual poverty…acknowledge, that all they have, or hope to have, is owing to" what? (See pg. 15) *The free grace of God." (pg. 15)*

22. What do we "leave behind" as we "comprehend in our heart of hearts that Jesus' great sacrifice eliminated once and for all our numerous affronts to God?" (See pg. 16) *"Our ugliness and deplorable sinful state." (pg. 16)*

23. What two realities must our hearts and minds grasp in this first Beatitude? (See pg. 17) *"Acknowledging His vast greatness and grasping our impoverished spiritual state." (pg. 17)*

24. According to Matthew Henry, why must we call ourselves poor?" (See pg. 18) *"Because we are always in want [in need] of God's grace, always begging at God's door, always hanging around His house." (pg. 18)*

25. According to Mr. Harris, what should be our spiritual opinion of ourselves? (See pg. 18) *"We are to be as children…weak, foolish, and insignificant."*

— THE GREAT SOUTHERN BAPTIST PREACHER, VANCE HAVNER, ONCE SAID, "HUMILITY IS NOT THINKING MEANLY (OR BADLY) OF ONESELF BUT RATHER IT MEANS <u>NOT THINKING OF YOURSELF AT ALL</u>." ISN'T THIS WHAT BEING POOR IN SPIRIT IS AS WELL — THE ABILITY TO SO UNDERSTAND OUR OWN SPIRITUAL POVERTY THAT WE LOOK ONLY AT THE MAJESTY AND GLORY OF GOD TO FIND TRUE SIGNIFICANCE IN LIFE RATHER THAN AT OURSELVES AND OUR ACCOMPLISHMENTS?

Application/Discussion Questions

Application Question #1: Review Fact questions 1-4. Describe in a few sentences your own journey through which you became aware of your own spiritual poverty and need of Jesus Christ.

Application Question #2: Review Fact question 6. In what ways do people sometimes become spiritually complacent? How can you tell whether you are spiritually enthusiastic enough not to be called lukewarm?

Application Question #3: Review fact questions 7-8. Explain the importance of the cross in our understanding of what it means to be poor in spirit.

Application Question #4: Review fact question 9. Mr. Harris makes it clear that possessing or not possessing "worldly treasures" is not a measure of our spiritual condition. Discuss some ways some have taught that worldly treasures are a 'sign' of God's favor.

Application Question #5: Review fact question 10. What does it mean to be *"totally destitute of wealth, influence, position, and honor, and being completely powerless to accomplish what one desires?"* Give at least one example of what that means to be destitute and what it doesn't mean.

Application Question #6: Review Fact question 11. Of what does this "free grace of God" consist, and how do you know you have received it?

Application Question #7: Review Fact questions 12-14. Understanding our wretched spiritual condition leads us to "hanging around" God's house. What do you think Mathew Henry meant by such a statement, and what does this "hanging around" God's house look like in your life?

Application Question #8: Answer the two "Thoughts for meditation" questions on page 22 of the book.

Scripture

Review the Scriptures concerning God's greatness and our spiritual poverty found on pages 22-23. Pick at least one in each category to memorize and write the passages here:

Note: You may pick other verses on these subjects if you like, but still write them below).

1.

2.

Chapter 3 – "Those Who Morn" – Pages 24-37

Fact Questions

26. Using a concordance or computer, find and read the account of Abraham and Isaac on Mount Moriah from the Scriptures. How does it relate to the Beatitude "Blessed are those who morn?" (see page 27 2nd Paragraph). *See Genesis 22:1-19 – "The message remains the same—to our sorrow and desperate cry—God always responds, just as he did to Abraham and Isaac." (pg. 27)*

27. When our lives are overcome by grief, sorrow, and despair, what is revealed about our relationship with God (and His relationship with us)? (See pg. 27). *The realness of our relationship with God is revealed. (pg. 27)*

28. What do the wails of grief among unbelievers reveal about their response to death? (See pg. 27) *They "reveal complete absence of hope to ever see their loved one again," and a "terrifying uncertainty of their loved one's destiny." (pg. 27)*

29. What is a believer assured of concerning his or her loved one who has died? (See pg. 27-28) *"That the departure of his or her loved one represents only a time of separation." (pg. 28)*

30. What does God provide for His children who are in the "darkest moments" on earth? (See pg. 28) *"Peace that passes all understanding" Philippians 4:6-7, and God's presence is with us as well. (pg. 28)*

31. What two assurances does God provide for the Christian concerning their Christian loved ones who have died? (See pg. 28) *That they were "transported to heaven at the moment of their departure from this world," and "A blessed reuniting with those who have preceded us and are now residents in our future heavenly destination." (pg. 28)*

32. What "profound pronouncement" did Mr. Harris' mother make to him shortly before her death? (See pg. 30) *"Death is normal" (pg. 30)*

33. Based on John 16:20, what does Mr. Harris say is "always" God's plan? (See pg. 30) *"To transform sorrow to consolation." (pg. 30)*

34. Besides to "death and tragedy," to what else does Mr. Harris say this second Beatitude applies? (See pg. 31) *"Remorse [we experience] from the diabolical attacks we must endure in our spiritual pilgrimage."(pg. 31)*

35. What is the "result" of our mourning in its essence? (See pg. 33) *It is "totally turning our burdens over to God with sincere faith that His consolation will carry us through whatever valleys we are experiencing." (pg. 33)*

36. What is the "consolation promised from the Lord" and what will be the result of our "calling upon him?" (See pg. 34) *The Holy Spirit who "will come and minister to your broken heart and renew your spirit to health as only he can do." (pg. 34)*

37. T/F _____ Waiting on God to work His will in our lives is a liberating experience that cultivates patience, dependence, and faith, and elevates us to a new level of life and living." (See pg. 35) *True (according to Mr. Harris) (pg. 35)*

38. From what does this "Beatitude for mourners" grant us freedom according to Mr. Harris? (See pg. 35) *Freedom from "the worry, want, and care of each day and enables us to live above life's circumstances." (pg. 35)*

39. For what purpose does God use the difficult circumstances in life? (See pg. 36) *"To purify us as a refining fire." (pg. 36)*

— GROUP DISCUSSION: WHAT DOES SIN HAVE TO DO WITH MOURNING IN THIS BEATITUDE? HOW MIGHT THIS BEATITUDE APPLY IN THE LIVES OF THOSE WHO ARE NOT CHRISTIANS BUT ARE "SEEKING" RELIEF FROM THEIR SIN? WHAT ARE SOME SPECIFIC WAYS YOU MAY COMFORT SOMEONE WHO IS "POOR IN SPIRIT" AND "MOURNING" OVER THEIR SIN?

Application/Discussion Questions

Application Question #1: Review fact question 1. What is the message that 'remains the same' and just how does the Lord respond to our sorrow and desperate cry?

Application Question #2: Review fact question 2. In your own words, describe what you understand to be a "real" relationship with God.

Application Question #3: Review fact question 3. What might you say to help comfort a non-believer who is mourning the death of a loved one?

Application Question #4: Review fact questions 4-6. What does the phrase "the presence of God with us" mean, how do you "experience" His presence as a Christian?

Application Question #5: Review fact question 7. Mr. Harris' mother rightly described death as 'normal' because all will face it. Read 1 Corinthians 15:54-58.

What is the ultimate 'fate' of death, and in what way may its 'normalcy' motivate us as Christians (see verse 58)

Application Question #6: Review Fact questions 8-9. Describe some ways that you or someone you know (or know about) has suffered and seen God transform sorrow to consolation.

Application Question #7: Review Fact question 10. What does it mean to turn over your burdens to The Lord in faith and how will you know you have believed "enough" for God to "carry you through whatever valley you are facing?"

Application Question #8: Review application question 11. How has the Holy Spirit ministered to YOUR broken heart in the past as you walked through difficulties?

Application Question #9: Review fact question 12. Do you believe there are different levels to achieve in the Christian life? Describe what you think a "new level of life and living" looks like.

Application Question 10: Review fact questions 13-14. Realizing that God often uses difficulties in life to refine us, how has this process granted you greater "freedom" from worry about the everyday affairs of life? If you are not currently increasing in this freedom, why do you think this is so?

Scripture

Review the Scriptures concerning God's comfort found on pages 36-37. Pick at least two verses to memorize and write the passages here:

Note: You may pick other verses on these subjects if you like, but still write them below).

1.

2.

Chapter 4 – "The Meek" – Pages 38-50

Fact Questions

40. Read the story of Moses related on pages 38-42. Who was doing the actual leading of the Hebrew people out of Egypt? (see page 42) *God (pg. 42).*

41. What, according to Mr. Harris, carried Moses "through the difficult assignment?" (see pg. 42) *Meekness (pg. 42)*

42. What were the consequences of Moses "lack of obedience "at the Springs of Moriah? (see pg. 43) *"He was punished and not permitted to set foot upon the Promised Land." (pg. 43)*

43. According to the author, it was Moses' meekness that "brought God's people to the Promised Land." What does he say led the people to "the impressive and eternal inheritance they still inhabit today?" (See pg. 43) *"Moses' obedient spirit." (pg. 43)*

44. What does Moses' life illustrate about meekness? (See pg. 43) *""Its power to make life effective in the Lord." (pg.43)*

45. What two aspects of Moses' character made a close relationship with God possible? (see pg. 43) *"Moses' absolute meekness before His Lord and his daily determination to fulfill God's instructions, whatever they might be." (pg. 43)*

46. Read the last paragraph of page 43. What two things "must we do" like Moses? (pg. 43)

    a. *"Daily seek God to direct and oversee our duties and encompass our planned and spontaneous interactions."*

    b. *"Desire that all our decisions be in accordance with His perfect purpose for us."*

47. 15. If we do these two things, what will be the result? (pg. 43)

    a. *"We can discover great encouragement and reward as we review the past."*

    b. *We can realize how God has used us in ways we never "contemplated.)*

    c. *God promises "much for those whose heart is right toward Him." ("He makes his steps firm (Ps. 37:23); planned (Ps. 85:13); unhindered (Prov. 4:12); surefooted, and confident (2 Sam. 22:43). (pg. 43)*

48. Describe the concept of meekness in the Old Testament, and in Moses' life. (See pg. 44) *In the OT meekness meant "To be wholly dependent on God to defend injustice." For Moses it was, "A total trust in God's goodness and control." (pg. 44).*

49. According to Mr. Harris, in the New Testament, Jesus "elevated meekness to a nobler status." How does the author describe Jesus 'meekness? (see pg. 44)? *As a fine blend of spiritual poise and strength from an intense inward spiritual awareness and direction. . . ." It is a life "characterized by deep eddies of patient strength of action and a quiet determination to do what must be done." (pg. 44)*

50. What does "such submission" as that described above "require?" (See pg. 44) *"Relinquishing all our selfish aspirations and enticements." (pg. 44)*

51. What must be the fate of "all ego? (see pg. 44) *It must be "impaled on the cross." (pg. 44)*

52. What two positive characteristics does meekness exhibit that we usually do not combine? How does the author define each one? (See pg. 44) *Strength which is inner toughness; and gentleness which is tenderness and care toward others. (p. 44)*

53. T/F _____ According to the author, "turning the other cheek" is about "allowing oneself to be brutalized by people who do not like you or agree with you." Explain your answer. (See pg. 45) *False – "It is about going forward and ignoring other people's distractions and deceptive attempts to deter you from achieving what you have set out to accomplish." (pg. 45)*

54. Break down the elements of meekness defined in Gill's quote. Meekness is:

   a. *Not easily [provoked] to anger.*
   b. *Patiently able to put up with [injuries] and affronts.*
   c. *To have the humblest]thoughts of oneself and the highest] thoughts of others*
   d. *Not caught up in [envy] of the gifts and graces of others.*
   e. *Willing for instructions and [admonitions]*
   f. *Willing to ascribe [all one has] to the grace of God*

55. According to the quote from John Gill on pages 45-46, what character trait equates with meekness? (see pg. 45-46) *"Humility." (pg. 45)*

56. What does Jesus promise to His followers as the end result of meekness? (see pg. 46) *"They will inherit the earth." (pg. 46)*

57. T/F _____ To inherit the earth means the meek shall obtain material wealth and power. Explain your answer. (see pg. 46) *False – "The meek have been especially prepared to establish God's kingdom on earth." ()pg. 46)*

58. Christ is the greatest of all examples of meekness (Phi. 2:6-11). What does our genuine meekness allow according to Mr. Harris? (see pg. 47) *"His light to come to full brilliance in us." (pg. 47)*

59. According to Mr. Harris, what is the "essence" of meekness for us? (see pg. 47) *"The crucifixion of our prideful nature." (pg. 47)*

60. What is the greatest temptation confronting those seeking meekness? (see pg. 48) *"SELF" (pg. 48)*

61. According to Mr. Harris, what is the key to finding victory over self? (see pg. 48) *"Surrender more and more of ourselves to allow His Spirit to be clearly visible in us." (pg. 48)*

— ESTABLISHING GOD'S KINGDOM ON EARTH IS PARTICIPATING IN "FILLING THE EARTH WITH GOD'S GLORY." FILLING THE EARTH WITH GOD'S GLORY MEANS FILLING THE EARTH WITH GOD'S RIGHTEOUS PEOPLE! HOW MIGHT AN ATTITUDE OF MEEKNESS BE AN ASSET IN ACCOMPLISHING THIS TASK? (SEE 1 PETER 3:15 AND 2 CORINTHIANS 5:20)

Application/Discussion Questions

Application Question #1: Review Fact questions 1-5. Describe the impact meekness plays for you in living an "effective" Christian life.

Application Question #2: Review Fact question 4. In what way does our obedience or lack of obedience contribute to our either gaining the victory or suffering punishment?

Application Question #3: Review fact question 6-8. Define "absolute meekness" and ""daily determination to fulfill God's instructions." How will you know you have achieved this absolute meekness and determination?

Application Question #4: Review fact questions 9-10. Describe the difference between meekness in the OT and in the NT. Which do you most naturally identify with and why?

Application Question #5: Review fact questions 11-12. Give an example of "selfish aspirations and enticements" you now face, or have faced in the past. What does it mean to "impale" these on the cross and how do you accomplish this?

Application Question #6: Review Fact question 13. What are some practical ways that strength and gentleness show themselves through meekness?

Application Question #7: Review Fact question 14. Give an example of "biblically" turning the other cheek as Jesus envisions it in the New Testament.

Application Question #8: Review fact questions 15-16. Evaluate your Christian walk in light of John Gills definition of meekness. Which one challenges you the most and why?

Application Question #9: Review fact questions 17-18. Give some 'practical' ways meekness helps us participate in building God's kingdom on earth.

Application Question 10: Review fact questions 19-22. On a scale from 1-5 with 5 being 'total' surrender – rate your level of surrender of self and the measure of the Holy Spirit/Christ's "brilliance" shining through your life.

Scripture

Review the Scriptures concerning meekness found on pages 49-50. Pick at least two verses to memorize and write the passages here:

Note: You may pick other verses on this subject if you like, but still write them below).

1.

2.

Chapter 5 – *"Those Who Hunger and Thirst After Righteousness"* – Pages 51-65

Fact Questions

62. What is Job's "sole possession' that, according to Mr. Harris, Job controls? (see page 52) *His faith (pg. 52).*

63. What is it that held Job's world together? (see pg. 52) *God's righteousness in him (pg. 52)*

64. What does the fourth Beatitude 'declare' to "all whose highest priority is to seek God's righteousness?" (see pg. 52) *"blessings and fulfilment." (pg. 52)*

65. According to the author, what is God's "greatest desire?" (See pg. 53) *"To fill his children with Himself." (pg. 53)*

66. What synonym for righteousness did Mr. Harris learn in language school that "burst upon [his] understanding?" (See pg. 53) *"Justice." (pg.53)*

67. What is the 'worthy goal' that this justice should produce in us? (see pg. 53) *People must work to, "be totally tuned in to God's wavelength and aspire that his ways become our way of thinking, making decisions, and forging the steps of our life." (pg. 53)*

68. What is the 'primary source' in acquiring a more intimate knowledge of God? (see pg. 54) *"The Word" in which he "reveals himself—his nature, his purposes, and his highest aspirations for us." (pg. 54)*

69. What is the "singular, mighty, and magnificent purpose" for which the Bible was written? (see pg. 54)

    a. *To comprehend God*
    b. *"to expose his millennial mission to redeem mankind"*
    c. *"to illustrate who his people were[Israel and the church]" (pg. 54)*

70. What are the "prerequisites" established in the first four Beatitudes that are "essential to acquire a ravenous hunger for God's righteousness?" (See pg. 54) *"Humility, dependence, and meekness." (pg. 54).*

71. Which Beatitude does the author say "has changed our inner perspective, values, and priorities? (see pg. 54)? *Meekness (pg. 54)*

72. What reveals our hearts truest desires?" (See pgs. 54-55) *"Our obedience."(pg. 54-55)*

73. What is "the primary expression of our love for God?" (see pg. 55) *"The submission of our hearts to God's commandments." (pg. 55)*

74. According to Mr. Harris, "In short, righteousness is _____

_____" (see pg. 56) *"everything that God requires and expects from his children, as revealed in the Scriptures. (pg. 56)*

75. According to Charles Fredrick Hogg and W E Vine, what is the only way to attain God's righteousness? (See pg. 57) *Our trust in Christ. (pg. 57)*

76. Again according to Hogg and Vine, what does "faith thus exercised" do for us? (see pg. 57) *It "brings the soul into vital union with God in Christ, and inevitably produces righteousness of life, that is, conformity to the will of God." (pg. 57)*

77. According to Mr. Harris, righteousness represents "who God is and what he requires of us." What else does righteousness represent? (see pg. 57) *"The One by whom this holy demand is accomplished and satisfied." (pg. 57)*

78. Man can never attain the holy righteousness of God, "but God made us righteous through Christ." What does this enable for us according to Mr. Harris? (see pg. 57) *"to conform to his perfect standard of holiness as new men." (pg. 57)*

79. The more of the "deep meanings of righteousness" we discover, what "greater realization" might we expect? (see pg. 57) *"A greater realization of all that Christ has done for us." (pg. 57)*

80. In what two ways can we find "giant treasure troves of righteousness" according to Mr. Harris? (see pg. 57) *"In God's written Word and in the living Christ." (pg. 57)*

81. What will be the result for those who truly hunger and thirst for goodness and holiness? (see pg. 58) *"They will be filled…experiencing an overflow of fattening from God's holiness and goodness." (pg. 58)*

82. According to Mr. Harris, what becomes the "principle driving force in our spiritual pilgrimage?" (see pg. 58) *"The atoning power of [Christ's] crucifixion and resurrection." (pg. 58)*

83. What does God use to "reveal us to ourselves? (see pg. 59) *"His Word" – see Hebrews 4:12. (pg. 58)*

84. What are the "rivers of living water" we experience as we thirst for righteousness? (see pg. 58) *"The Holy Spirit's presence." (pg. 58)*

85. For what must we "perpetuate a *stay hungry* diet even as we are filled to overflowing each day?" (see pg. 59-60) *The Word of God. (pg. 59)*

— THINK ABOUT AND DISCUSS THE FOLLOWING COMMENT: THE FIRST FIVE BEATITUDES ARE WRITTEN PRIMARILY TO THOSE WHO ARE NOT YET CHRISTIANS, BUT ARE SEEKING GOD. THEY DESCRIBE THE JOURNEY TO CONVERSION AS A PERSON REALIZES HIS SPIRITUAL BANKRUPTCY, MOURNS OVER HIS SIN, REALIZES HIS OWN INABILITY TO CORRECT HIS WAY, AND TURNS TO GOD ALONE TO FILL HIS LONGING FOR RIGHTEOUSNESS AND RECONCILIATION WITH GOD. HAVING RECEIVED CHRIST'S RIGHTEOUSNESS BY FAITH, HE CAN REJOICE THAT HE WILL NEVER BE MORE RIGHTEOUS IN GOD'S EYES BECAUSE OF THE 'DEEPER' LEVEL OF HIS LONGING FOR RIGHTEOUSNESS, OR HIS GROWING PERSONAL OBEDIENCE IN THIS LIFE.

Application/Discussion Questions

Application Question #1: Review Fact questions 1-2. What is the connection between our faith and God's righteousness? (See Ephesians 2:8-10).

Application Question #2: Review Fact question 3. Decide now and declare: Is God your highest priority in life right now? How did you come to that conclusion?

Application Question #3: Review fact questions 4-6. As you understand God's justice, what does it mean to be "be totally tuned in to God's wavelength and aspire that his ways become our way of thinking, making decisions, and forging the steps of our life?" How will you know you have 'totally tuned in' to God?

Application Question #4: Review fact questions 7-8. Give some practical suggestions on how best to use the Word of God to increase your knowledge of God and to better fulfill His purposes?

Application Question #5: Review fact questions 9-12. Discuss the place of humility, meekness, dependence, obedience, and submission plays in the journey toward righteousness?

Application Question #6: Review Fact questions 13-16. Define righteousness as used here, and state clearly how this righteousness is both obtained and maintained.

Application Question #7: Review Fact question 17. Explain some ways (give examples) of how you or someone you know and respect have "conformed" to God's "perfect standard of holiness."

Application Question #8: Review Fact questions 18-21. Realizing what Christ has done for us through His finished work as revealed in His Word, *how* does this realization inform and impact your relationship(s) with God and with other people?

Application Question #9: Review Fact question 22. What central fact or facts does God's Word reveal about all of us that directly impacts our ability to obtain righteousness? (See Romans 3:10-11; 5:12; Galatians 3:10).

Application Question 10: Review Fact questions 23-24. In light of the answers to both these questions, how do you personally experience the Holy Spirit's presence?

Scripture

Review the Scriptures concerning righteousness found on page 62. Pick at least two verses to memorize and write the passages here:

Note: You may pick other verses on this subject if you like, but still write them below).

1.

2.

Chapter 6 – "The Merciful" – Pages 66-85

Fact Questions

86. List Peter's actions on pages 66 to the top of page 72 separately in the space below. (see pages 66-72).

   a. <u>Cutting off the servant's ear in the Garden</u> – pg. 66
   b. <u>Sleeping instead of praying in the Garden</u> – pg. 67
   c. <u>Refusing to allow Jesus to wash his feet</u> – pg. 67
   d. <u>Resisting Jesus' calling initially</u> – pg. 68
   e. <u>Jumping out of the boat amidst the angry waves and then sinking</u> – pg. 68
   f. <u>Confessing Jesus as "the Christ, the Son of the Living God!</u> – pg. 68
   g. <u>Rebuking Jesus for saying that He, Jesus, must die</u> – pg. 69
   h. <u>Promising to never leave Jesus no matter what, and then denying Him 3 times</u> - pgs. 69-71
   i. <u>Went with John to Jesus' tomb after the resurrection</u> – pg. 72

87. What did Jesus do in light of Peter's "great remorse?" (see pg. 72) *Jesus sought Peter out in order to comfort him. (pg. 72)*

88. What were the results of Jesus' actions for Peter? (see pg. 72-73) *Peter was "ready to be the bedrock of faith, to serve in power and boldness, and to make the mercy of Christ known to his entire generation!" (pg. 72-73)*

89. T/F _____ Even if we stray from God, or betray Him like Peter, God's mercy will find us. Explain you answer. (see pg. 73) *True (pg. 73)*

90. What is God's mercy proof of according to Mr. Harris?" (See pg. 73) *Of God's unconditional love. (pg. 73)*

91. Why do all of us, "desperately require his [God's] mighty restoring mercy to move us forward in life…?" (See pg. 73) *Because we all commit great sin. (pg. 73)*

92. Read the words to the song, "Come Back Home" on page 73. To what biblical parable does the song allude? *The parable of the Prodigal Son. (pg.73)*

93. What sentiment does Mr. Harris say is closely linked and easily confused with mercy, and what is the difference between the two? (see pg. 74) *Pity which is 'sorrow for someone's plight' is different from mercy which is 'the deep inward urge to do good for a person, even at personal expense and sacrifice.' (pg. 74)*

94. Read the story of "Stickman" from Mr. Harris' time in Bangladesh. How did "Stickman" react to the Danish relief workers merciful offer to take him back to Denmark and restore him to a normally functioning life? (see pgs. 74-76). *He refused the offer (pg. 76)*

95. Like "Stickman" with the Danish relief offer, what offer do many people refuse to accept from the Lord? (see pg. 76) *The free gift of salvation. (pg. 76)*

96. What must WE do to bring results from God's offered mercy? (See pg. 76) *"we must accept it [God's offer of mercy]" (pg. 76).*

97. 11. What do "so many people not understand" about their spiritual condition? (see pg. 77)? *That "they are abject beggars before the God of the universe... [they are] "vagabonds before God." (pg. 77)*

98. 12. How is mercy defined according to W. E. Vine? (See pg. 77) *"to feel sympathy with the misery of another, to have compassion abiding in one's heart, to show kindness by benevolence, to help the afflicted, and to bring help to the wretched." (pg. 77)*

99. Even when we were blindly unaware of our own sin, what did God, who is rich in resources, do for us? (see pg. 77) *He rescued us. (pg. 77)*

100. How did He rescue us? (see pg. 77) *"He sent Jesus to pay our price, seek us out, and save us once for all."(pg. 77)*

101. What "two mercies" do the beatitudes involve according to Mr. Harris? (See pg. 77) *"The first is the wondrous mercy to help those in need, and the second is the mercy that compels us to incarnate the same mercy toward others." (pg. 77)*

102. T/F _____ Mr. Harris believes that, as Christians, we are infused with God's unconditional love and therefore cannot help but reveal His mercy to others. (see pg. 77) *True (pg. 77)*

103. What was the "simple gripping message" that Mr. Harris learned as a boy in church in Alabama that he credits with truly changing his life? (see pgs. 78, 79) *That Jesus wanted him and not [or rather than] his "years of ineffective efforts to live a life good enough to please Him." (pg. 78)*

104. From what did God's mercy free Mr. Harris? (see pg. 79) *"from a works mentality." (pg. 79)*

105. What does Mr. Harris now 'fully' understand? (see pg. 79) *"[T]hat Jesus was the full and complete sacrifice for my sins" and that he must "share His mercy with others."(pg. 79)*

106. What is Jesus' "mercy gift of love to us to make us alive in his spiritual realm?" (pg. 80) *His "willingness to undergo terrible torment" for us. (pg. 80)*

107. What is "the symbol of God's great love gift" to those who "wander in unbelief and ignorance?" (see pg. 80) *It is the Cross of Christ. (pg. 80)*

108. Like the woman caught in adultery, Jesus shows mercy to each of us, though we too are sinners. It is a mercy that is "completely unearned, and cannot be paid back." What is it's "divinely designed" purpose? (see pgs. 81-82) *"to make us whole and complete before God." (pg. 82)*

109. According to Mr. Harris, what does "each person" have the "opportunity" to do about God's mercy? (see pg. 82) *"to reject or accept it." (pg. 82)*

— **ONE OF THE MORE IMPORTANT DISTINCTIONS BETWEEN MERCY AND GRACE IS THAT MERCY INVOLVES THE WITHHOLDING OF JESUS IN HIS CAPACITY AS JUDGE, CONDEMNING THE SINNER, WHO IS NOT PUNISHED BECAUSE OF GOD'S MERCY. GRACE, ON THE OTHER HAND, INVOLVES THE POURING OUT OF CHRIST AND ALL HIS BLESSINGS TO THE UNDERSERVING — TO YOU AND ME!**

Application/Discussion Questions

Application Question #1: Review Fact questions 1-4. What possible differing reactions might some people have to Jesus' granting His mercy to sinners like Peter?

Application Question #2: Review Fact question 2. What factor do you think Peter's remorse had on Jesus' decision to grant Peter mercy?

Application Question #3: Review fact questions 4-5. Where would you 'draw the line' at showing mercy to someone who has 'strayed from God,' or even 'betrayed' Him like Peter? In what way is God's 'unconditional love' truly unconditional?'

Application Question #4: Review fact questions 6, 7, and 12. What is the central problem between God and man that these three questions are pointing to, and what can YOU do about it?

Application Question #5: Review fact question 8. What is the difference between mercy and pity? Give a practical example of the difference.

Application Question #6: Review Fact question 9-11, 14-15. What is your understanding of what a person must do to receive mercy? How does that apply practically in day to day life?

Application Question #7: Review Fact questions 13, 16, and 17. What are some ways that Christians can show mercy today, and what is the source of that mercy?

Application Question #8: Review Fact question 18. Briefly describe a time when you personally realized that God wanted you rather than your behavior.

Application Question #9: Review fact questions 19-24. Understanding that God's mercy is His gift through the Person and work of His Son Jesus Christ, what are some specific ways you can His mercy to others?

Application Question 10: Review the text box on the distinction between mercy and grace. Do you agree with the distinction? Why or why not? What are the implications of this distinction, if any, on the practice of mercy in our lives today?

Scripture

Review the Scriptures concerning mercy found on pages 83-85. Pick at least two verses to memorize and write the passages here:

Note: You may pick other verses on this subject if you like, but still write them below).

1.

2.

Chapter 7 – *"The Pure in Heart"* – Pages 86-108

Fact Questions

110. Read the account of David's life given on pages 86-92. What were the promised consequences of David's years of sinfulness, and how are those consequences characterized? (see page 92). *"The sword shall never depart from your house, and I [God] will rise up evils against you from your own household." These consequences are described as 'harsh but just.' (pg. 92)*

111. According to Mr. Harris, what does David's 'powerful example' convey to us? (see pg. 92) *That even those whose "hearts are right toward God" are "capable of stumbling headlong into terrible mistakes." (pg. 92)*

112. What indicates the "true measure of our relationship with God" in the aftermath of such sinful behavior? (see pg. 92) *"Our brokenness and desire for restoration." (pg. 92)*

113. Harris writes, "God sees our heart, forgives our sin, and restores our relationship with him." What does God first 'survey' before restoring that relationship? (see pg. 92) *"just how desperate our desire for Him is." (pg. 92)*

114. In our battle with 'self,' what does the pure in heart person attempt to do with 'self?' (See pg. 93) *To "keep self crucified…and impaled on the cross." (pg. 93)*

115. What is "public enemy number one" to the pure in heart? (See pg. 93) *Self. (pg. 93)*

116. What will God 'examine' in His throne room when we stand before Him? *"Our spiritual heart."(pg.93)*

117. For what does God "continually search" according to Mr. Harris? *For "pure, undefiled hearts that are right toward him." (pg. 94)*

118. Read the first full paragraph on page 94. List in the spaces provided below, the description of our hearts given in this paragraph. (see pg.94).

    a. *Our heart houses our values*
    b. *It is the decision center of right and wrong for us*
    c. *It determines our behavior*
    d. *It determines how we relate to others.*
    e. *It directs our thought life and what we dwell on*
    f. *It empowers our personality and who we are toward others*
    g. *It dictates our decisions in life, both good and bad*

119. What will God reveal about us in His throne room once He strips away all the pretense and excuses in our lives? (see pg. 94) *"The true nature of our being." (pg. 94)*

120. How is the word "pure" used in the Greek in reference to the heart? (See pg. 94) *As, "a sincerely genuine, innocent, and blameless heart; a heart free from corrupt desire, sin, and guilt; a heart purified by fire and free of defilements of the flesh and the world; and a clear and transparent heart. A pure heart is solely and wholly committed to [pleasing] God in all one thinks, does, and says." (pg. 94).*

121. According to Mr. Harris, what is "the great blessing of this beatitude? (See pg. 94) *"growing in our knowledge of God."(pg. 94)*

122. Mr. Harris describes Noah as one who was pure in heart, and who was 'totally committed' to God. What was it that ultimately "paid off" for Noah, his family, and us? (see pg. 95) *Noah's obedience and daily dedication to God's plan in the face of ridicule." (pg. 95)*

123. What was it about Abraham's life that demonstrated a pure heart? (see pgs. 95-96) *Abraham's faithfulness. (pg. 96)*

124. Why did Mary 'receive the awesome privilege' of becoming Jesus' mother? (See pg. 96) *"Because of her humble and faithful heart." (pg. 96)*

125. To what do these biblical examples, and others, such as Enoch, Elijah, Moses, and Paul inspire us? (see pg. 96) *To "seek an ever higher level of fellowship with our Lord and Savior." (pg. 96)*

126. For what future benefit will "those developing pure hearts here on earth" be "much more prepared?" (see pg. 97) *"For heavenly citizenship in God's eternity." (pg. 97)*

127. According to Mr. Harris, what must we understand to "achieve and maintain a pure heart?" (see pg. 97) *The way Satan attacks and how to defend ourselves from those attacks. (pg. 97)*

128. What allows us to maintain purity in this world? (see pg. 97) *"The mighty power of God in us." (pg. 97)*

129. What else must we be 'aware of' and what else must we do if we are to maintain pure hearts?" (pg. 97) *"We must be aware of sin so we can confess it and have it washed away in the blood of Christ to restore our cherished relationship with the Lord." (pg. 97)*

130. What three different parts in our human nature composed of according to Adrian Rodgers? (see pg. 98) *Body, soul, and spirit. (pg. 98)*

131. What "seat of temptation" primarily attacks our body? (see pgs. 98) *"our sinful nature." (pg. 98)*

132. What seat of temptation attacks our soul which is "our psychological, emotional, and intellectual seat?" (see pg. 98) *"The world" (pg. 98)*

133. Where does Satan attack our spirit? (see pg. 98) *"In the arena of our pride and self-sufficiency. (pg. 98)*

134. How do we combat these three major areas of temptation? (see pg. 98-99)

    a.   Against the flesh we are to: *Flee (pg. 98)*

    b.   Against the world we must: *exercise faith (pg. 98)*

    c.   Against the temptations of the spirit we are to: *fight (pg. 99)*

135. What does Mr. Harris say that our "business with God" depends on entirely? (see. Pg. 100) *"the condition of our heart." (pg. 100)*

136. What are the "great impediments to acquiring a clean heart?" (see pg. 102) *"Uncleanness and impurity." (pg. 102)*

137. What will it take for us to "pass the test" of a pure heart before God? (see pg. 102) *"Only when our heart is fully exposed and bathed in Jesus' holy and healing radiance is the true measure of our sanctification revealed before Him." (pg. 102)*

138. T/F _____ Achieving a pure heart is not a painful exercise. Explain your answer. (see pg. 102) *False – it is "painful because it forces us to deal with deep rooted issues." (pg. 102)*

139. What can we not "knowingly ignore" if we are to maintain a clean heart? "(see pg. 106) *"Any unresolved relationship." (pg. 106)*

— **TO MAKE YOU THINK**

— **WHEN YOU BECAME A CHRISTIAN BY TRUSTING CHRIST, WHICH OF YOUR SINS WERE FORGIVEN AT THAT TIME?**

— **A. THE ONES COMMITTED BEFORE YOU TRUSTED CHRIST ONLY**

— **B. THOSE SINS AND THE ONES YOU COMMIT AFTER TRUSTING CHRIST**

— **NOW – WHAT IS THE PREREQUISITE FOR HAVING YOUR SINS FORGIVEN AFTER TRUSTING CHRIST?**

— **A. I MUST FIRST CONFESS THOSE SINS FOR THEM TO BE FORGIVEN.**

— **B. THERE IS NO PREREQUISITE BECAUSE ALL MY SINS ARE FORGIVEN – PAST – PRESENT – AND FUTURE IN CHRIST**

Application/Discussion Questions

Application Question #1: Review Fact questions 1-2. What point do you think Mr. Harris is making by reviewing David's sinfulness?

Application Question #2: Review Fact question 3-8. Describe in your own words what you think a 'pure heart' looks like, and how you will know when you have 'attained' such a heart. Just how 'desperate' do you actually have to be for God to listen to you?

Application Question #3: Review fact questions 9-11. After reviewing all the elements of a pure heart mentioned in this section, on a scale of 1-10, with 10 being the most pure, and one the least pure, rate the present purity of your own heart. Explain your answer.

Application Question #4: Review fact questions 12-16. What is the "higher level of fellowship with the Lord" that these pillars of the faith attained? Are you living at that level now? If not, what changes do you need to make to reach such a level of maturity in the Lord?

Application Question #5: Review fact questions 18-24. Just how does the "Mighty Power of God" overcome the impurity of our hearts and lives? What will it take for you to 'tap into' this power in your own life?

Application Question #6: Review Fact question 25. Give one example in each of the three categories where you were able to overcome the temptation of the world, the flesh, and the Devil. How were you able to succeed?

Application Question #7: Review Fact question 26. Describe your present relationship with God in terms of your heart. Are you close to Him, far away, or not really sure? What will it take for you to draw closer to Him?

Application Question #8: Review Fact question 27. What areas challenge you most in trying to maintain a pure heart before God?

Application Question #9: Review Fact questions 28-29. In the final analysis, what will it REALLY cost you to attain to, and then maintain, a pure heart before God?

Application Question 10: Review Fact question 30. For your personal application. Write down the name of anyone in your life with whom you have a broken relationship. Make specific 'plans' to restore those relationships as quickly as possible (See Matthew 5:23, 24 & Matthew 18:15-17).

Scripture

Review the Scriptures concerning purity found on page 108. Pick at least two verses to memorize and write the passages here:

Note: You may pick other verses on this subject if you like, but still write them below.

1.

2.

Chapter 8 – "The Peacemakers" – Pages 109-129

Fact Questions

140. Read the account of Joseph's life given on pages 109-118. Through all that Joseph suffered, from his brother's selling him into slavery, to Potiphar's wife, and time in jail; who or what does Joseph tell his brothers was behind all his suffering, and why? (see page 117). *""God sent me [Joseph] here before you to preserve life, to preserve for you a remnant of the earth, and to keep you alive by a great deliverance. Now, it was not you who sent me here, but God." (pg. 117)*

141. Who is the true peacemaker, to whom did he provide reconciliation, and how was that reconciliation accomplished? (see pg. 118) *God, who reconciled man to Himself through Jesus Christ. (pg. 92)*

142. As believers, what are we "compelled to pursue passionately?" (see pg. 118) *"a ministry of reconciliation with all those in conflict around us." (pg. 118)*

143. What does Mr. Harris say are the "basic building blocks for effective peacemaking?" (see pg. 118) *"Goodness, righteousness, and truth" (pg.118)*

144. What book of the Bible does Mr. Harris say is "rich in practical peacemaking?" (See pg. 119) *Proverbs (pg. 119)*

145. What two biblical commands impact our ability to express 'normal' human reactions like "gossiping, arguing, fighting, and criticizing' others? (See pg. 119) *Phil. 2:3 which says, "Do nothing out of selfish ambition or vain conceit. Rather, in humility value others above yourselves." And, Matthew 5:45, "Love your neighbors, and pray for those who persecute you in order that you might be sons of your Father in heaven." (pg. 119)*

146. Read Matthew 5:39-41. What does Mr. Harris indicate was Jesus' purpose in telling his followers to 'turn the other cheek' and to 'go' the extra mile? (see pgs. 119-120) *Such actions provide "an opportunity...for the believer to share about God's grace in Christ." (pg.120)*

147. What does Mr. Harris say is, "love personified and is the distinguishing mark of a follower of Christ?" (see page 120) *Peace (pg. 120)*

148. In what practical ways did Pedro, the heart transplant recipient, demonstrate the reality of his conversion to Christ? (see pgs.120-121). *He, "visited from house to house, pleading forgiveness for his former hostile actions, returning items he had stolen." And he invited his neighbors to a Bible study in his home. (pg. 121)*

149. No matter where we are 'planted,' what will "Christ in us" press for? (See pg. 122) *"restoration of relationships and reconciliation of individuals to one another."* *(pg. 122).*

150. What does Mr. Harris say is, "a worthy, challenging admonition, and is an ideal place to initiate peacemaking? (see pg. 122) *"The building up of others."* *(pg. 122)*

151. Since 'self-less' obedience is not really possible through human 'strength or intentions,' where must we turn to 'execute' the high command to be peacemakers; what source has God given to assist us in becoming peacemakers? (see pg. 122) *"Only the grace and force of God in us can yield such spiritual results." The fruit of the Spirit is the source. (pg. 122)*

152. How do we "assimilate these traits [fruit of the Spirit] into our daily life?" (see pgs. 122-123) *"By 'more of God and less of me' living." … "God's increased presence within empowers you to practice peacemaking, not in your strength but in the strength and direction of the Holy Spirit." (pgs. 122-123)*

153. What else do peacemaking situations depend on to "identify solutions and provide counsel?" (pg. 123) *"heavenly wisdom." (pg. 123)*

154. List the 'four G's of peacemaking recommended by Peacemaker Ministries. (pgs. 123-124) *Glorify God, Get the log out of your own eye, Gently restore the relationship, Go and be reconciled.*

155. What "G" underlies all the others?" (see pg. 124) *"The Gospel of Jesus Christ"* which is *"what motivates every authentic peacemaker." (pg. 124)*

156. Who is the only one who "truly transforms lives and reconciles broken relationships? (see pg. 124) *Only Jesus. (pg.124)*

157. What "unlimited potential" does a peacemaker have in Christ? (see pgs. 126-127) *"to affect lives and decisions of those individuals in our path. We can alter devastating destinies and direct souls into the peace of pardon, power of purpose, and eternal communion with our Lord." (pgs. 126-127)*

158. As God's children, what responsibility does Mr. Harris say is ours? (see pg. 127) *"God's reconciling mission in this world is who we are!" (pg. 127)*

159. Read the 'peacemaker' account of the woman at the gas station on page 127. What was Mr. Harris' point in using this story? (see pg. 127) *"If we are not responsive to God's prompting and direction to be peacemakers, often no one else is there to do it." (pg. 127)*

Application/Discussion Questions

Application Question #1: Review Fact questions 1-2. When, and under what circumstances, did you experience God's reconciling work in your own life?

Application Question #2: Review Fact question 3. What compels YOU to passionately pursue reconciliation with others? What tends to prevent you from seeking reconciliation with others?

Application Question #3: Review Fact question 4. Do you agree or disagree with this statement? Briefly explain how 'goodness, righteous, and truth' apply to 'effective peacemaking.'

Application Question #4: Review Fact questions 5-7. Using the scripture indicated in these questions, explain why peacemaking is needed and how 'turning the other cheek,' or 'going the extra mile' might impact your attempts at peacemaking.

Application Question #5: Review Fact questions 8-9. What are some practical ways you have seen that gain a 'hearing' for the Gospel of peace similar to Pedro's experience?

Application Question #6: Review Fact questions 10-11. These questions are moving toward the quest for personal reconciliation with others. Describe ways you personally have been able to 'build up others' that has led to reconciliation and peace.

Application Question #7: Review Fact questions 12-14. Mr. Harris rightly believes that the power to become a peacemaker must originate in God through the ministry of the Holy Spirit. He also believes that in order to receive or exercise that power "we must decrease and He must increase." Question: How will you know when you have decreased enough, or He has increased enough for you to become an 'effective' peacemaker? What 'steps' should you take to help foster this greater dedication to our Lord?

Application Question #8: Review Fact questions 15-17. How does the Gospel inform, guide, and impact your peacemaking ministry?

Application Question #9: Review fact question 18. Describe an occasion when you, or someone you are aware of, were able to positively affect someone else's life toward greater peace with God or with other people.

Application Question 10: Review fact questions 19-20. What is your understanding of God's 'prompting' in your own life, that (if you 'listened' better), might help you to become a more faithful peacemaker?

Scripture

Review the Scriptures concerning peacemaking found on page 128-129. Pick at least two verses to memorize and write the passages here:

Note: You may pick other verses on this subject if you like, but still write them below.

1.

2.

Chapter 9 – "The Persecuted" – Pages 130-144

Fact Questions

160. Read the crucifixion account on pages 130-132. What fate, endured by Jesus, will many peacemakers face? (see page 132). *Persecution by the very people they try to help. (pg. 132)*

161. What separates the "persecution of the blessed from others suffering persecution?" (see pgs. 132-133) *"The cause—for righteousness sake, those who are persecuted because they refuse to renounce…God in their lives." (pg. 133)*

162. What does "identity with Jesus in this world' sometimes bring to the Christian? (see pg. 133) *"unjust persecution." (pg. 133)*

163. What does Mr. Harris say is the "supreme goal of our [Beatitude] quest?" (see pg. 133) *"to become more and more like our Lord and reflect His image in every way." (pg.133)*

164. What is the "subsequent result of being a peacemaker?" (See pg. 133) *Persecution (pg. 133)*

165. What does Mr. Harris conclude will cause the peacemaker to be "the odd man out?" (See pg. 134) *"Man's sinful nature, his warped reasoning, and his adversarial relationship to God."(pg. 134)*

166. For what, according to John Gill, are Christians persecuted? (see pg.134) *for their righteous and godly behavior which brings upon them the hatred and enmity of men." (pg. 134)*

167. What are the various 'kinds' of persecution Christians might expect according to John Gill? (see page 134) *by the tongue, through cruel mocking and reproachful language, or by repression, banishment, imprisonment, and innumerable sorts of death." (pg. 134)*

168. Who are the 'spiritual wine tasters' of this, 'sweetest wine, of persecution?' (see pg.135). *"those who are fully aware of the spiritual richness and reward in which they are about to imbibe and for which they are willing to sacrifice themselves."(pg. 135)*

169. What, according to Mr. Harris, will "striving to live set apart for God" bring to the Christian? (see pg. 137) *"attention to oneself.... If you're going to be a faithful follower of Christ in your actions, thought, and conviction, people will take notice." (pg. 137)*

170. On pages 137 and 138, Mr. Harris gives several examples of "decision-points" that "clearly display how well we live for God." List his examples below:

a. *"How will you begin your day? By clicking on the news or seeking communion with the Lord?" (pg. 137)*

b. *Travelling to work, will you "listen to the morning radio shows…or turn to music or message that will inspire and focus you on Jesus for the day?" (pg. 137-138)*

c. *During the day, "do you participate in gossip, or do you edify those around you?" (pg. 138)*

d. *"Do you plunge right into your midday meal or offer a word of grace while others stare?" (pg. 138)*

e. *"Do you respond to a frustrating person with irritation and pride, or do you offer the offender grace and/or words of forgiveness?" (pg. 138)*

171. What is "required" of us, "from the very first to the final Beatitude? (see pg. 138) *"a total surrender to God, his will, and direction." (pg. 138)*

172. If we "delight in living for Christ," what might we expect from the world? (see pg. 138) *Persecution (pg. 138)*

173. T/F _____ Severe persecution will make us bitter and "derail us from a purposeful life in Christ." Explain your answer. (pg. 138) *False. (pg. 138)*

174. How does God use the "terrible tragedy" of the martyred pastor in Bangladesh? (pgs. 140) *Eventually, the murders came to Christ because of the unconditional love showed them by the pastor's family. (pg. 140)*

175. Acknowledging that the "Precipices of Persecution" are "precarious" subjecting us to a possible fall, instead of looking "down to see the great expanse before us," what does Mr. Harris teach is the solution for this dilemma? (see pg. 141) *""We are to fix our eyes above on Jesus. (pg. 141)*

176. What makes the severe cost of persecution worth it in this world? (see pg. 141) *"Making a difference for Christ." (pg.141)*

177. According to Mr. Harris, our peacemaking has "propelled us to this plane of living" where we are enabled to die daily or even to die physically for our Lord. What does he say 'we are to be' for Christ? (see pg. 141) *"crusaders and heroes for Christ." (pg. 141)*

178. Amazingly, what has the journey through the Beatitudes prepared us for? (see pg. 142) *"to finally experience our heavenly reward." (pg. 142)*

179. Besides preparing us for our heavenly reward, and fellowship with Jesus, what has He done for us here on earth through these Beatitudes? (see pg. 142) *Made us more beautiful and useful for Christ here on earth. (pg. 142)*

- **PERSECUTED CHRISTIANS**
- **EACH MONTH:**
- **322 CHRISTIANS ARE KILLED FOR THEIR FAITH.**
- **214 CHRISTIAN CHURCHES AND PROPERTIES ARE DESTROYED**
- **772 FORMS OF VIOLENCE ARE COMMITTED AGAINST CHRISTIANS**

THE TOP FIVE COUNTRIES PERSECUTING CHRISTIANS:

1. **NORTH KOREA**
2. **SOMALIA**
3. **IRAQ**
4. **SYRIA**
5. **AFGHANISTAN**

SOURCE: **https://www.opendoorsusa.org/christian-persecution/** MAY 24, 2015

Application/Discussion Questions

Application Question #1: Review Fact questions 1-3, 5. Describe a time when you personally, or someone close to you, has suffered persecution unjustly for righteousness sake.

Application Question #2: Review Fact question 4. What are some ways we can reflect the image of Jesus in our lives?

Application Question #3: Review Fact questions 6-8. What are some ways that unbelievers demonstrate their hatred of those committed to Christ?

Application Question #4: Review Fact question 9. What exactly is the spiritual richness and reward that those who suffer persecution for the Lord's sake can expect?

Application Question #5: Review Fact question 10. Give some specific examples of 'actions, thoughts' and convictions' that, as a 'faithful follower of Christ' would cause people to take notice.

Application Question #6: Review Fact question 11. What other examples might you give to "clearly display how well [you] live for God?"

Application Question #7: Review Fact question 12. What does it mean to totally surrender to God, His will, and direction, and how will you know you have achieved this total surrender

Application Question #8: Review Fact question 13. What does it mean to "delight in living for Christ" in such a way that it will result in persecution?

Application Question #9: Review Fact questions 14-17. What are some specific ways God has used persecuted Christians to "make a difference for Christ?"

Application Question 10: Review Fact questions 18-20. Describe someone you know who has been made more beautiful in Christ through applying these beatitudes in their lives, and you might call a crusader and hero for Christ.

Scripture

Review the Scriptures concerning persecution found on page 143-144. Pick at least two verses to memorize and write the passages here:

Note: You may pick other verses on this subject if you like, but still write them below.

1.

2.

SONG TITLES AND ALBUM REFERENCES (INCLUDED ON POWER-POINTS) BY LESSON

1. Treasures from Jesus—The Beatitudes**, Children Ensemble, *The Beatitudes Life* (Introductory Lesson)
2. "Amazed,"** Kutless, *It Is Well* (Poor in spirit)
3. "Face Down,"** Casting Crowns, *Come to the Well* (Poor in spirit)
4. "Yesterday," Charlie Hall, *The Rising* (Poor in spirit)
5. "The Splendor of My King,"** Bucky Heard, *The Beatitudes Life* (Poor in Spirit)
6. "Carry Me to the Cross," Kutless, *Believer* (Those who mourn)
7. "The Well,"** Casting Crowns, *Come to the Well* (Those who mourn)
8. "Everything I Need,"** Kutless, *It Is Well* (Those who mourn)
9. "My Heart Will Break No More,"** Annette Herndon, *The Beatitudes Life* (Those who mourn)
10. "So Far to Find You,"** Casting Crowns, *Come to the Well* (The meek)
11. "Less of Me,"** Bucky Heard, *The Beatitudes Life* (The meek)
12. "Lamp,"** Charlie Hall, *The Rising* (Hunger and thirst for righteousness)
13. "Close to You,"** Beyond the Ashes, *The Beatitudes Life* (Hunger and thirst for righteousness)
14. "Constant,"** Charlie Hall, *The Rising* (Between the Beatitudes)
15. "Come Back Home,"** Kutless, *Believer* (The merciful)
16. "Mercy,"** Casting Crowns, *Until the Whole World Hears* (The merciful)
17. "Micah 6:8,"** Charlie Hall, *Flying into Daybreak* (The merciful)
18. "When Mercy Came,"** Annette Herndon, *The Beatitudes Life* (The merciful)
19. "My Own Worst Enemy,"** Casting Crowns, *Come to the Well* (Pure in heart)
20. "At Your Feet,"** Casting Crowns, *Until the Whole World Hears* (Pure in heart)
21. "Center,"** Charlie Hall, *Flying into Daybreak* (Pure in heart)
22. "Make Me Pure,"** David Staton, *The Beatitudes Life* (Pure in heart)
23. "Jesus, Friend of Sinners,"** Casting Crowns, *The Well* (Peacemakers)
24. "Vessel of Peace,"** Babbie Mason, *The Beatitudes Life* (Peacemakers)

25. "This Is Love,"** Kutless, *Believer* (Persecuted) (optional-see CD reference)
26. "Hero,"** Kutless, *Believer* (Persecuted)
27. "Already There,"** Casting Crowns, *Come to the Well* (Conclusion)
28. "Song of the Redeemed,"** Charlie Hall, *Flying into Daybreak* (Conclusion)
29. "The Beatitudes Are Your Beauty in Me,"** Annette Hearndon, Bucky Heard, David Staton, Babbie Mason, *The Beatitudes Life* (Conclusion)

ALBUM INFORMATION

Casting Crowns

Come to the Well. 2011, Sony/Atv Tree Pub (BMI), compact disk.
Until the Whole World Hears. 2009, Sony/Atv Tree Pub (BMI), compact disk.

Charlie Hall

The Rising. 2010, EMICMGPublishing.com, compact disk.
The Bright Sadness. 2008, EMICMGPublishing.com, compact disk.
Flying into Daybreak. 2006, EMICMGPublishing.com, compact disk.

Kutless

Believer. 2012, Simpleville Music, Inc, compact disk.
It Is Well. 2009, EMICMGPublishing.com and Simpleville Publishing, LLC, compact disk.

The Beatitudes Life

2014, DirksWorks, Inc, compact disk

THE STORY AND OTHER MUSIC VIDEOS

Videos from *The Story* Copyright 2011, Big Book Media: ©2011 EMI Christian Music Group, Inc., Provident Label Group LLC, a division of Sony Music Entertainment, Word Entertainment, LLC. All rights reserved.

1. "Your Heart" by Chris Tomlin (about King David) (Introduction and Pure in heart lessons)
   http://www.youtube.com/watch?v=2O-m6GxEX2o
2. "Detail of the Universe: This Will Blow Your Mind" with "Amazed" and "God of Wonders" by Kutless (Poor in spirit)
   http://www.youtube.com/watch?v=1jeGIUKvWNw&feature=youtu.be
3. "Who but You" by Mark Hall and Megan Garrett (About Abraham) (Those who mourn)
   "The Story" video not available on YouTube (lyrics only)
4. "It Must Be You" by Bart Millard (about Moses) (The meek)
   http://www.youtube.com/watch?v=nDQdzksTCaQ
5. "Broken Praise" by Todd Smith (about Job) (Hunger and thirst for righteousness)
   "The Story" video not available on YouTube (lyrics only)
6. "When Love Sees You" by Mac Powell (about Jesus) (Merciful)
   http://www.youtube.com/watch?v=l2zHk95UnsE
7. "How Love Wins" by Steven Curtis Chapman (about the Thief on the cross) (Persecuted for righteousness sake)
   http://www.youtube.com/watch?v=hHOG2Ktqoe0
8. "Move in Me" by Jeremy Camp (about Paul) (Conclusion)
   http://youtu.be/cB-x1has8Vo

This music video listing with YouTube links is also available on the website: questforthebeatitudes.org

SOURCES

Lesson 2: Blessed are the poor in spirit.

1. Gill, John. 1980. *An Exposition of the Old and New Testaments (Complete)*. Grand Rapids, Michigan: Baker Books. *http://www.biblestudytools.com/ commentaries/ john-gill-complete/matthew 5:3*. Accessed July 2011-March 2012.
2. LaHaye, Tim and Jenkins, Jerry. 2007. Used by permission of G. P. Putnam's Sons, a division of Penguin Group (USA) Inc.

Lesson 3: Blessed are those who mourn.

1. Hunt, T. W., and King, Claude N. 1995. *The Mind of Christ*. Nashville, Tennessee: Lifeway Press. Reprinted and used by permission.

Lesson 5: Blessed are those who hunger and thirst after righteousness.

1. Henry, Matthew. 2006. *Matthew Henry's Commentary on the Whole Bible (Complete and Unabridged in 6 Volumes)*. Peabody, Massachusetts: Hendrickson. *http://www.biblestudytools.com/commentaries/matthew-henry-complete/Matthew 5:6*. Accessed July 2011-March 2012.
2. Hall, Charlie. *The Lamp*. Copyright 2010, worshiptogether.com Songs (ASCAP) sixsteps Music (ASCAP) EMICMGPublishing.com, compact disk. International copyright secured. All rights reserved. Used by permission.

Between the Beatitudes

1. Hall, Charlie. *Constant*. Copyright 2010, worshiptogether.com Songs (ASCAP) sixsteps Music (ASCAP) EMICMGPublishing.com, compact disk. International copyright secured. All rights reserved. Used by permission.

Lesson 7: Blessed are the pure in heart.

1. Strong, James. 1977. *Strong's Exhaustive Concordance of the Bible*. Nashville, Tennessee: Thomas Nelson. *http://www.blueletterbible.org/lang/lexicon/Strongs/kathros (pure)*. Accessed July 2011-March 2012.
2. Rodgers, Adrian. 2005. Chapter 5: "How to Handle Temptation." In *What Every Christian Ought to Know*. 87-109. Nashville, Tennessee: Broadman & Holman Publishers. Reprinted and used by permission.
3. Robertson, Archibald T. 1932-33; renewed, 1960. *Robertson's Word Pictures in the New Testament*. Nashville: Broadman Press. *http://www.biblestudytools.com commentaries/robertsons-word-pictures/purity*. Accessed July 2011-March 2012. Reprinted and used by permission.

Lesson 8: Blessed are the peacemakers.

1. Sande, Ken. 2004. *The Peacemaker: A Biblical Guide to Resolving Personal Conflict*. Grand Rapids, Michigan: Baker Books. Reprinted and used by permission.

Lesson 9: Blessed are those persecuted for righteousness' sake.

1. Gill, John. 1980. *An Exposition of the Old and New Testaments (Complete)*. Grand Rapids, Michigan: Baker Books. *http://www.biblestudytools.com/commentaries/john-gill-complete/matthew 5:10-12*. Accessed July 2011-March 2012.
2. Hunt and King 1995, 211.
3. LaHaye and Jenkins 2007, 214-215.

Lesson 10: Conclusion

1. Bergman, Brian; Hall, Charlie; Ragland, Dustin; Combes, Kendall; and Anderson, Quint. "Song of the Redeemed." Copyright 2006, worshiptogether. com Songs (ASCAP) sixsteps Music (ASCAP) EMICMGPublishing.com, compact disk. International copyright secured. All rights reserved. Used by permission.

BEATITUDES SONGS
WITH YOUTUBE LINKS

"Amazed" by Kutless
http://www.youtube.com/watch?v=O8TP9uvapUQ (Poor in spirit)

"Face Down" by Casting Crowns
http://www.youtube.com/watch?v=7gLDr1K zuk (Poor in spirit)

"Yesterday" by Charlie Hall
Not available on YouTube (Poor in spirit)

"Carry Me to the Cross" by Kutless
http://www.youtube.com/watch?v=C0UeOSrTEAs (Mourn)

"My Brightness" by Charlie Hall
http://www.youtube.com/watch?v=jr4Fcj0it1E (Mourn)

"The Well" by Casting Crowns
http://www.youtube.com/watch?v=vLxdxw4Gj6g (Mourn)

"Everything I Need" by Kutless
http://www.youtube.com/watch?v=211y1hH8EnI (Mourn)

"Carry On" by Kutless
http://www.youtube.com/watch?v=DqkAnWxbamU (Meek)

"So Far to Find You" by Casting Crowns
http://www.youtube.com/watch?v=GwWPVRjB49U (Meek)

"Lamp" by Charlie Hall
http://www.youtube.com/watch?v=-O4ENKX9XbA (Hunger and thirst)

"Constant" by Charlie Hall
http://www.youtube.com/watch?v=dSDE2Yf5q1I (Between the Beatitudes)

"Come Back Home" by Kutless
This recording not available on YouTube (Merciful)

"Mercy" by Casting Crowns with video clips from the gospel of John http://www.youtube.com/watch?v=wP0mNZ1K2aY (Merciful)

*****Version with lyrics recommended for the Beatitude Moment of The Merciful*****
http://www.youtube.com/watch?v=31xJ0qd1WJU

"Micah 6:8" by Charlie Hall
http://www.youtube.com/watch?v=n4xmPuMXnL4 (Merciful)

"My Own Worst Enemy" by Casting Crowns
http://www.youtube.com/watch?v=tvmu1JuDHCI (Pure in heart)

"At Your Feet" by Casting Crowns
http://www.youtube.com/watch?v=yT6lFcM-Fv8 (Pure in heart)

"To Know You" by Casting Crowns
http://www.youtube.com/watch?v=P4xp6ygQoAo (Pure in heart)

"Center" by Charlie Hall
http://www.youtube.com/watch?v=KE3HKym0tRE (Pure in heart)

"Jesus, Friend of Sinners" by Casting Crowns
http://www.youtube.com/watch?v=66zqQBxhUDA (Peacemakers)

"This Is Love" by Kutless
http://www.youtube.com/watch?v=mMSKZaUunlo (Persecuted)

"Hero" by Kutless
http://www.youtube.com/watch?v=fwAF96mFQqE (Persecuted)

"All We Need" by Charlie Hall
http://www.youtube.com/watch?v=mvTfuHpd3ys (Conclusion)

"Already There" by Casting Crowns
http://www.youtube.com/watch?v=qrOotpSKOX0 (Conclusion)

"Song of the Redeemed" by Charlie Hall
http://www.youtube.com/watch?v=vcexvlx2JPo (Conclusion)

This song listing with YouTube links is also available on the website: questforthebeatitudes.org